I KNOW YOU GOT SOUL

I KNOW YOU GOT SOUL

Machines with That Certain Something

JEREMY CLARKSON

MICHAEL JOSEPH
an imprint of
PENGUIN BOOKS

MICHAEL JOSEPH

Published by the Penguin Group
Penguin Books Ltd, 80 Strand, London WC2R 0RL, England
Penguin Group (USA) Inc., 375 Hudson Street, New York, New York 10014, USA
Penguin Books Australia Ltd, 250 Camberwell Road, Camberwell, Victoria 3124, Australia
Penguin Books Canada Ltd, 10 Alcorn Avenue, Toronto, Ontario, Canada M4V 3B2
Penguin Books India (P) Ltd, 11 Community Centre, Panchsheel Park, New Delhi – 110 017, India
Penguin Group (NZ), cnr Airborne and Rosedale Roads, Albany, Auckland 1310, New Zealand
Penguin Books (South Africa) (Pty) Ltd, 24 Sturdee Avenue, Rosebank 2196, South Africa

Penguin Books Ltd, Registered Offices: 80 Strand, London WC2R 0Rl, England

www.penguin.com

First published 2004
4

Copyright © Jeremy Clarkson, 2004

The moral right of the author has been asserted

Set in Din and T-Series
Designed and typeset by Smith & Gilmour, London
Printed in Great Britain by Butler and Tanner, Frome, Somerset

A CIP catalogue record for this book is available from the British Library

ISBN 0-718-14729-4

This book is dedicated to my children, Emily, Finlo and Katya, who had to walk round the house on tiptoes, and not listen to Radio One, while it was being written.

ACKNOWLEDGEMENTS

I'd like to thank my wife, who helped by locking the children in the cellar for three months and by agreeing that Radio One should not be played when 'Daddy's trying to write'. I'd also like to thank Rowland White at Penguin, who never shouted at me once.

CONTENTS

INTRODUCTION

I suppose the inspiration for this book came from my reaction
to the Concorde crash in Paris.

Normally when a plane goes down we mourn for the people on
board, but on this occasion I found myself mourning, most of all, the
death of the machine. How could something so wondrous and dazzling
have come to grief? It really was as shocking as the death, just down
the road, in fact, of Princess Diana.

The fact is that most machines are just a collection of wires and
plastic. The computer, for instance, on which I've written this book
has no more of a heart than a Toyota Corolla, which in turn is no
more soulful than a Corby trouser press.

But some machines do have a soul. Sometimes, as is the case with
Concorde and the AK47, it's because they possess that most human of
qualities, a flaw, and sometimes it's because they were born carrying
the genetic fingerprint of a foolish and misguided inventor. Count
Zeppelin springs to mind here.

Whatever, just about all the machines here have formed the
backbone of some incredible stories, none more so than the Spitfire.
Of course we remember 'the few' whose bravery held back the Nazi
hordes in that balmy summer of 1940. But, secretly, we know that
much of their success was attributable to the incredible speed and
manoeuvrability of the aeroplane they flew.

And yes, before you raise an eyebrow, I know all about the Hurricane
but it lacks the film-star looks somehow, and the glamour. And anyway,
I can't pretend this book is a comprehensive list of all the machines
ever made with a soul. Nor is there any scientific basis for the choices.
My editor and I simply went out for lunch one day and came up with

a list on the back of a napkin. They were machines we liked, picked for emotional reasons, using our hearts rather than our heads.

The hard part was choosing which machine from a particular genre should be singled out. All battleships, for instance, had soul by the bucketful principally because they were flawed and usually useless, but there was only space here to look at one so I went for the biggest. And most useless of them all – the astonishing *Yamato*.

The next difficult bit was choosing what to leave out. The Gibson Les Paul should be here, I know, but unfortunately, before I had the chance to include it the producer of *Top Gear* rang and said I really must get back to the bothersome business of making television programmes.

Sorry.

CONCORDE

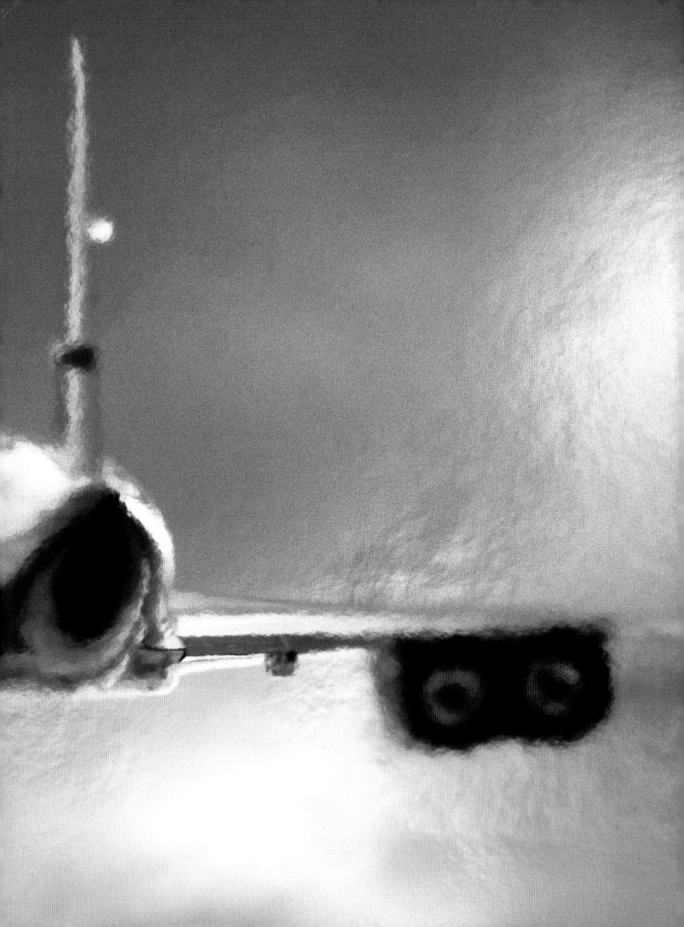

There was much brouhaha when the last Concorde touched down at Heathrow in the summer of 2003. Television stations went live to the scene, tears were shed and commentators talked about how it was the end of an era. And yet in the midst of all this were a handful of Guardianistas saying 'good riddance'.

They pointed out that Concorde had cost £2.1 billion to design, which, even though this was the sixties, made it three times more expensive than the Dome. And with little specks of spittle at the corner of their mouths, they went on to remind everyone that for years the great white bird was, in fact, a great white elephant.

The taxpayer had met the cost of building it, and for many, many years they'd had to dig even further into their pockets to run it. And who benefited? Well, according to those of a sandal persuasion, it certainly wasn't the ordinary working man in the street. No. It was a bunch of fat capitalist corporate raiders going to New York to do another deal that would make life even less pleasant for the poor sods who'd paid for the plane in the first place.

If you squint a bit, it is possible to see the logic in this argument. But if you open your eyes, then I'm afraid it makes no sense at all. Concorde was indeed extremely useful for those who make and break companies and countries for a living. You could sell GEC and GM over breakfast in London and then, over a second breakfast in New York, buy Guatemala and Chad.

But for these people it was only a tool, a time-saving device, like an electric razor or a toaster. And from inside the plane it really wasn't anything special. There was no shortage of legroom but the seats were no wider than the seats you get on a National Express coach, and headroom was pinched too.

What's more, because of the weight, passengers were denied even the basic frills that are commonplace in cattle class these days. Yes, the wine was fine, and free, but there was no in-flight movie system, no little map telling you where you were, no video camera in the nose wheel. You spent three hours in a seat with nothing to do but devise a plan for buying Peru while staring at the bald patch of the man in front, who was trying to bankrupt Poland.

CONCORDE FLEW AT 60,000 FEET, WHICH IS TWICE AS HIGH AS A 747 GOES.

Exciting? You'd think so, wouldn't you, tearing through the stratosphere at Mach 2, but actually it wasn't exciting at all. Sure, there was a meaty kick on the runway but it was no more thrustful than a BMW 330i. And there was a satisfying surge as the tail cleared Cornwall and the pilot lit the afterburners to break through the sound barrier. But you could get more of an adrenalin rush on any fairground ride.

Far, far below, people crossing the Atlantic on boats would hear the sonic boom and yet on board there wasn't even a judder as the sound barrier was breached, and there was no view either. People say you could see the curvature of the earth but really it was no more pronounced than it is from the beach. And nor was it black or purple up there because, contrary to popular belief, you were not on the edge of space. You were not even halfway there.

Concorde flew at 60,000 feet, which is twice as high as a 747 goes, and that sounds impressive. But 60,000 feet is only 11 miles and that, when you remember the moon is 98,000 miles away, is not really very far at all.

So, on the upside Concorde was quick and comfortable because it did fly above the turbulence. But on the downside it was cramped, boring and so noisy in the back that Michael Winner and Roger Moore would have fist-fights over who'd get seat 1A where it was only deafening.

I flew on Concorde twice. Once when I was given an upgrade and once as a guest on its final flight from New York. I never paid for a ticket and I never wanted to because I never saw it as a tool. For me, watching Concorde was so much better than being on it.

This is the point the Guardianistas missed. They thought the ordinary miner and nurse had paid for Concorde and derived no benefit. But we did. Because we were the ones on the ground, pointing . . .

For eighteen years I lived in Fulham, slap bang in the middle of the flight path into Heathrow, and as a result I never once heard the second item on either the six or the ten o'clock news. Every night, at 6.03 and 10.03, the gentle hum of London would be drowned out by the immense crackling thunder of those four Olympus engines. And every night I'd go to the window to watch the source of this roar slide by.

In Barbados all the planes are made to fly miles from the coast so they don't disturb the holidaymakers. But Concorde was allowed to come right down the beaches of the West Coast, skimming the palm trees with its broken nose, the jet wash rippling the sand. To watch the Americans wetting themselves with excitement over the spectacle – and it was pure theatre – made me almost gooey with pride.

£2.1 billion? Bah! It was cheap.

It was a scientist with NASA who summed up Concorde better than anyone I've ever met. 'Putting a man on the moon was easy,' he said, 'compared to getting Concorde to work.'

First of all there were the political hurdles. To get Armstrong onto the lunar surface NASA simply furnished a bunch of German rocket scientists with a lot of American dollars and sat back to reap the rewards. But over here we had no German scientists. They refused to come here after the war because it was felt we didn't have enough money.

They were right. We had the bones of an engine but not the funds to build a plane. So in 1962 we had to join forces with the French, who had the bones of a plane but no engine. This meant France and England

Every night, at 6.03 and 10.03, the gentle hum of London would be drowned out by the immense crackling thunder of those four Olympus engines. And every night I'd go to the window to watch the source of this roar slide by.

FLYING AT MACH 2 GENERATES MASSIVE HEAT, SO MASSIVE THAT CONCORDE GROWS BY SEVEN INCHES IN FLIGHT.

would have to work together. And that's a bit like Arsenal teaming up with Manchester United. Macmillan and de Gaulle fell out after about seven minutes. No one could even agree about how Concorde should be spelled – with or without the 'e'.

It was Tony Benn, the then minister for science and technology, who pushed the deal forward, forcing the French to sign a 'no-get-out clause'. This meant that, no matter what, they would be required to stick with the project and not pull out leaving the British taxpayer holding the billion-dollar albatross.

It sounded like a good idea at the time because you can't trust Johnny Frog. However, as the years rolled by, it was a succession of shaky British governments who wanted out but couldn't because of Benn's clause in the contract.

Meanwhile the engineers were hard at work. Now you have to remember that this was a time when top-loading washing machines were considered advanced. There were no CD players or push-button phones. There were computers, but they were the size of houses and took all day to get through the seven-times table. So Concorde was going to be designed by men, with pencils.

It seemed like a truly impossible dream. There were fighter jets capable of getting through the sound barrier, but they only had a range of fifteen minutes at full power and they were flown by RAF pilots who sat on ejector seats and needed oxygen masks. What's more, after one sortie the planes would need weeks of maintenance.

So the idea of building a plane that could fly all the way to America faster and higher than any fighter, and then turn round and come straight home again, seemed ludicrous, especially as the people inside would be wearing lounge suits, rather than g-suits.

The main problem was the atmosphere. When a plane is travelling subsonically it parts the air easily, but when it goes up past Mach 1 the air no longer knows it's coming and does not part. It smashes into the leading edges of the plane with such force that people on the ground, miles below, can actually hear it being rent asunder. This is the sonic boom.

This collision creates massive heat, so massive that Concorde really does grow by seven inches in flight. On one early trip across the Atlantic a pilot put his hat in a space between two bulkheads and was alarmed to find on landing that the bulkheads were joined together more tightly than two coats of paint. Not until the return leg, when the plane had swelled up again, could he get his hat back, although by then it was more a mortar board really.

Some of the heat that generated this expansion transferred itself into the cabin. There was one part of the dashboard that was hot enough at Mach 2 to double up as a frying pan. The tiny windows were hot to the touch. And 10 per cent of the power produced by the engines had to be used to juice the air conditioners.

It was the heat that screwed the Americans. Like the British and French, they never foresaw millions of holidaymakers paying £99 for trips to Florida with Freddie Laker. Flying, for 50 years, had been the preserve of the rich, and as a result they thought the future lay beyond Mach 1.

Unfortunately, they felt Mach 2 wasn't fast enough, and with their SST project aimed for Mach 3. That's what finished them. They tried

A scientist with NASA
summed up Concorde
better than anyone
I've ever met. 'Putting
a man on the moon was
easy,' he said, 'compared
to getting Concorde
to work.'

This unique formation of four Concordes took
weeks of planning to set up. Flying over the south
coast of England, each jet carried 65 passengers.

and tried, but at the time neither the technology nor the materials were available to get them past the drawing board. As a result they gave up and designed the Boeing 747 instead. Subsonic, cheap transport for the masses. Well, you never know. It might work ...

The Russians, too, developed a supersonic passenger plane that did actually fly. Into the ground. At an air show.

But even before this mishap Concordski was doomed because it had a range of just 1,500 miles, which would get it from Moscow to a point exactly 300 yards from the middle of nowhere. Technically it was clever because it could do Mach 2.2, like its European rival. Commercially it wasn't going anywhere, so Ivan jacked it in.

The British and French, however, did not give up. I have seen film of the engineers throwing an endless succession of paper darts down the wind tunnel at Bristol as they struggled to work out which shape worked best.

The second problem, after the heat, is that the supersonic shockwave has a nasty habit of sitting on the trailing edges of the wings, causing the ailerons to jam. It was this that caused a number of Spitfires to crash in the Second World War. In a dive, without realising it, the pilots were getting awfully close to Mach 1 and as a result they were dealing with forces they couldn't comprehend. What they could comprehend, in their last moments before they hit the ground, was that for no obvious reason the controls had jammed.

It was boffins at the Miles Aircraft Corporation who figured this one out, and knew the key to supersonic flight was to lose the ailerons. The whole wing had to move. Or you needed a delta wing as was used on the Vulcan bomber, and eventually Concorde. But the shape of that wing had to be precise because, and this is not an exaggeration, life on the far side of the sound barrier is the most hostile place on earth. Mach 1 makes the Arctic Ocean or the Sahara Desert look like Battersea Park.

And if the forces were troublesome enough for the plane, they were a complete nightmare for the engines. Because if you let the spindly blades of a jet crash into the air at Mach 2, they will shatter and that will be that.

WHEN CONCORDE WAS TRAVELLING AT 1,500 MPH THE AIR GOING INTO THE ENGINES WAS ONLY MOVING AT 500 MPH. HOW DO YOU DO THAT?

So the plane would be travelling at 1,500 mph, but the air going into the engines could only be moving at 500 mph. How do you do that? Well, you need to have paid attention in your physics lessons, that's for sure.

As the engineers toiled away the marketing men were having even bigger problems because of Concorde's range. It was better than a fighter, and better than the Russian attempt. But it was never going to be able to cross the Pacific and even the Atlantic was a struggle. It could get to New York from London or Paris, but not from Frankfurt. This meant the number of routes it could fly was limited, and that meant the number of airlines that might buy it was equally small.

And then, after the Yom Kippur War and the subsequent oil crisis, the number dwindled from sixteen to just two. The national carriers of the countries involved. So although the engineers surmounted all the technical problems, no outsider wanted to buy their creation.

And to make matters worse, the Americans, spiteful because their supersonic plane had come to nought, invented all sorts of reasons why it should not be allowed in their air space. Farmers even argued that it would knock over their cows.

In the end just fourteen Concordes were made, the last going to Air France for just £1, and the only place you could fly to from London was Bahrain. Absurd. The greatest technological achievement of all time and no one could find a use for it.

Eventually the Americans caved in, and later still British Airways even worked out how their white elephant could be turned into a cash cow. Passengers were asked how much they thought their ticket had cost – each had PAs and assistants to deal with travel agents so they didn't know – and amazingly most guessed way above the actual price. So BA simply matched the cost to the expectation.

It seemed that Concorde's future was assured. Compared to normal planes, which bounce around the world's airports like they're on speed, BA's flagship had a very small workload. There were very few landings and take-offs. And very little time spent in the air so there was quite literally no end in sight. Concorde would keep going until another visionary kick-started a project to build a replacement.

But then one of them crashed.

There had been near misses before. Tyres had burst, sending chunks of rubber into the wings. And on one notable occasion a BA plane had damn nearly run out of fuel coming into land at Heathrow. It actually conked out while taxiing to the terminal building.

None of these incidents had really made the news. After the fuel scare BA's publicity department said that the plane was at a different angle on the ground than it is in the air and that actually there was enough left in the tanks to keep the engines running for 20 minutes.

As a result it made a small story in just one newspaper. But, in fact, while it had enough fuel for 20 minutes' taxiing, there was only enough left for 90 seconds of flight.

The pilot, it turned out, had refused to slow down or refuel at Shannon when both his co-pilot and engineer realised something had gone wrong. He was sacked even before he could bash his hat back into shape.

The crash in Paris, though, made headlines everywhere and not just because of the casualties, who were mostly German. No, for the first

time since the *Titanic* we were actually mourning the loss of the machine itself.

As the weeks wore on scientists realised a burst tyre had punctured one of the fuel tanks and that, somehow, the fuel on board had caught fire. They took steps to make sure it couldn't happen again but the writing was already on the wall. And what little confidence was left went west after the World Trade Center thing.

Richard Branson made a few noises about taking the planes off BA's hands and making them work with Virgin logos on the tail fin, but this was ridiculous. The French had already announced there would be no airworthiness certificates any more, and Beardy knew that even if there were, BA would never relinquish their flagships. He was turning the slow death of Concorde into a PR stunt. And I'll never forgive him for that.

Concorde, you see, represented the greatness not just of the British and French boffins who'd made it against all the odds but also the sheer wondrous genius of the human race. This plane served as a twice-daily reminder that nothing was beyond us. Given time, and money, we could do absolutely anything.

Which is why, as I walked off the plane for the last time, I remember thinking, 'This is one small step for a man. But a giant leap backwards for mankind.'

You see, unlike any other machine that is mothballed or donated to a museum, Concorde has not been replaced with something better or faster or more convenient.

This, and I'm trying not to exaggerate, is a bit like discovering fire and then snuffing it out because someone got burned. Or finding America and not bothering to go back in case one of the ships sinks. Not since the Romans left Britain in AD 410 has mankind shied away from technological or social advance, until now. And that is the main reason, I think, why there was so much shock at Concorde's passing. Because it represented a sea change in the way we are.

We went to the moon and now we're on our way to Mars. We invented the steam engine and immediately replaced it with internal combustion. We went to Mach 1 and then we went to Mach 2. We went across the Atlantic in three hours . . . and now we can't any more.

And then there's the fate of the machine itself. For more than twenty years it was woken in the morning and flown to New York. And then one day no one came to replenish its tanks or vacuum its carpets. There was a big party and the next day . . . nothing. Imagine doing that to your dog. Putting it in a kennel one night and never going back.

It's a machine, so it can't possibly know about the crash or the problems of getting an airworthiness certificate. It was built to do a job and it did that job, faultlessly, for year after year. So why, it must be thinking, do they not want me any more?

Of course, we'll still be able to go and see the old girl in a museum. That'll be strange though. Going to a museum to see the future. Except, of course, Concorde isn't the future. It's the last, tumultuous, nail-biting chapter of the past.

When the car came along, we didn't shoot our horses. They became playthings, toys for huntsmen and twelve-year-olds at gymkhanas. And it's the same story with air travel.

Now we have the internet and video conferencing, big business can buy and sell its countries and its companies without ever leaving the swivel chair. There's no need to fly to America.

So the only reason for using a plane is because you want to go on holiday. And given the choice of going to Florida at Mach 2 or for £2, most would opt for the cheaper option.

Concorde, then, had to die not because it was too fast but because, in the electronic age, it was too slow.

ROLLS-ROYCE

As I write a car is sitting outside my window, waiting to be tested. I do not know where it is made or what it is called. I think it might be a Kia but it could be a Daewoo.

Whatever it is, you would find more character in a glass of water and more heart in an office rubber plant. And there's a very good reason for this.

In order for a car to have personality, an X factor, the company that makes it must be able to take guidance and inspiration from one man, the man who started the company in the first place.

This did not happen with the car outside my window, which was undoubtedly built in a jungle clearing by a company that makes cars to make money. No one began Proton or Hyundai or Daewoo because they'd harboured a dream of making something extraordinary or special. These are just enormous engineering and construction conglomerates that have been told by their respective governments to make cars so that the locals can get off their oxen and get modern.

We see the same sort of thing in Japan. There never was a Mr Toyota who, since he was a small boy, yearned for the day when he could build a small family hatchback that never broke down. And you can scour the history books until the sky turns green but you'll not find any mention of a young Timmy Datsun who stayed up until ten o'clock, even on school nights, devising his plan for a car with two milometers.

Subarus are made by a romantic-sounding outfit called Fuji Heavy Industries. At night I bet the chairman sometimes forgets he has a car division. It'll be just another entry in his plofit and ross accounts.

The only Japanese cars with even a trace of humanity are Hondas, and there's a very good reason for that. There was a Mr Honda and he did have a vision when he was a small boy. Even today that vision still steers the engineers, and as a result there's a very definite correlation between the S2000 sports car and those early motorbikes. It's solely because of this link with the past that I like Hondas more than any other Japanese cars.

Of course, in Europe most car firms were started by a visionary. Lotus was kick-started by Colin Chapman, who liked things light and frothy. Jaguar was the brainchild of Sir William Lyons, who liked comfort and speed, with a low, low price. Enzo Ferrari wanted to make cars solely to support his beloved race team.

Most of these guys, and others like them, are remembered by sound-bite quotes. Ettore Bugatti, for instance, once said, 'Nothing is too beautiful or too expensive.' Enzo Ferrari came up with 'the customer is not always right'. And Colin Chapman summed up his philosophy thus: 'Simplify and add lightness.'

Mind you, he also said, 'You would never catch me driving a race car that I have built.' Which probably explains why Lotus came to be known as an acronym for Lots Of Trouble, Usually Serious.

These men are all now dead, or in South America, but their DNA is still evident in the cars that are being made today. The Lotus Elise is light and breaks down a lot. The new Bugatti Veyron will be astoundingly expensive and I think the paddle-shift gearbox in a Ferrari 575 is silly. But what do I know.

Unfortunately, however, time does have a nasty habit of blurring the idealism that gave rise to these companies. I'm not sure, for instance, that Herr Porsche would get much of a hard-on for the Cayenne. And how would William Lyons react, I wonder, if he knew Jaguar's current board was chasing euros by offering a front-wheel drive, diesel-powered estate car? Sure, it may help Jaguar out of a small hole now, but by losing sight of the goal, the vision, it will drive them into a bigger one later. I grew up, for instance, wanting an E-type. But my son is not growing up yearning for the day when he can buy an X-type diesel.

There is, however, one car company out there that has never lost sight of its role in the market place. Rolls-Royce.

Sir Henry Royce, who founded the company back in 1904, really was a one-man quote machine. 'Strive for perfection in everything you do.' 'Accept nothing as nearly right or good enough.' 'The quality remains long after the price is forgotten.' 'Whatever you can do, or dream you can, begin it.'

You get the picture. And so did BMW. When they bought the company they could have fitted a new body to one of their 7 series.

I could not feel the road passing by through vibrations in the wheel and I could not hear the engine, big and V12-ish though it was. I have had long soaks in the bath that were more stressful.

ROLLS-ROYCE

"The Best Car in the World"

ROLLS-ROYCE, LIMITED
14 & 15 CONDUIT STREET, LONDON, W.

Telegrams:
ROLHEAD, LONDON
(Regd.)

Telephone:
GERRARD 1654 (3 lines)

PARIS ∴ NEW YORK ∴ PETROGRAD AND BOMBAY

Sir Henry Royce, who founded the company back in 1904, really was a one-man quote machine. 'Strive for perfection in everything you do.' 'Accept nothing as nearly right or good enough.' 'The quality remains long after the price is forgotten.' 'Whatever you can do, or dream you can, begin it.'

That's what Mercedes did to create the Maybach. But instead of wandering around the BMW spare-parts division saying, 'What do we want?' the engineers fired up their computers and asked, 'What do we need?'

Plainly they looked at what Henry Royce and Charles Rolls were trying to achieve a hundred years ago, and thought, 'Zis is vot ve must do also.' And as a result the Phantom is quite simply the best car in the world.

Obviously, it is not the easiest car in the world to park and nor, thanks to a top speed of 150 mph, is it the fastest. I should also draw your attention at this point to the handling, which is not what you'd call sporty. Unless, of course, your everyday transport is a hovercraft.

In my experience it is not the best-built car in the world either. It's not handmade – that's another way of saying the door will fall off – but it is hand-finished, and that's the next worst thing.

I heard, even before the car was launched, that on an advertising photo shoot the flying lady refused to come out from her cavity in the radiator grille. On *Top Gear* the same thing happened. And then, when I drove a Phantom to Hull, I came out of my hotel in the morning to find the statuette had hibernated and wouldn't come out for love nor money.

I rang a man at Rolls who did his best to sound surprised. 'The Spirit is stuck down?' he said, with an almost pantomime level of incredulity. 'That's never happened before.' Yeah right.

Inside the car BMW made a decision you might not like. Instead of festooning the cabin with a myriad of knobs and buttons, they are all hidden away in cubbyholes. You get a gear lever that allows you to go forwards and backwards, and that's it. You get a version of the BMW i-Drive computer with most of the functions removed. And most of the time the computer and satellite-navigation screen are hidden behind a perfectly normal, analogue clock.

As a result it's no more daunting in there than in a Georgian drawing room. You sit on a supremely comfortable chair – it'd be even better if it were a wingback, I'm surprised it's not – overlooking acres of leather

INSTEAD OF FESTOONING THE CABIN WITH A MYRIAD OF KNOBS AND BUTTONS, THEY ARE ALL HIDDEN AWAY IN CUBBYHOLES. YOU GET A GEAR LEVER THAT ALLOWS YOU TO GO FORWARDS AND BACKWARDS, AND THAT'S IT.

and wood. You're never tempted, as you are in the Maybach, to push a button just to find out what it does. And then having to spend the rest of the journey trying to find which button undoes whatever it is the first button did.

This makes for a hugely relaxing drive. So relaxing, in fact, that you sometimes forget that you're in a car.

I did. I was trundling up a motorway the other day, doing 60 mph, in a long snake of other cars, also doing 60. Only, unlike any of the other drivers, I could not feel the road passing by through vibrations in the wheel and I could not hear the engine, big and V12-ish though it was. I have had long soaks in the bath that were more stressful. I have been on tropical beaches that are more noisy.

After a while I became so detached from reality that I put on my indicator and tried to overtake the car in front. Sounds fine except for one thing. I was already in the outside lane. I came within an inch of hitting the central crash barrier and to this day I wonder what on earth the chap in the car behind felt when he saw a three-ton, £250,000 Rolls-Royce indicate, to show the driver wasn't asleep, and then drive off the road.

The radiator grille is bigger than my
first flat, and you could quite easily
have a game of cricket on the bonnet.
You could have a very major crash
in a Phantom and simply not know.
There's also a sense of imperiousness,
a sense that you really are driving
round in Queen Victoria.

RCC 398

I'd like to think he nodded sagely, turned to his passenger and said, 'My, to have detached the driver so completely from reality that must be a well-engineered car.' But I suspect he probably said, 'What a twat.'

That's the thing about driving a Phantom. You could pull over and give someone the entire contents of your wallet, and they'd look at you like you'd just given them the entire contents of your stomach. Stop at a junction to wave someone out and instead of a cheery wave you get a sneery V sign. On the pavement you are a normal person with ears and a spleen. In a Rolls you are the bastard love child of Fred West and Harold Shipman.

I quite like that. I like it because it shows cars, despite the best endeavours of Kia and Hyundai and Daewoo, are still able to raise the blood pressure a bit. It's good that nothing more than a mass-produced collection of iron ore, rubber, sand, cow skin and petrochemical by-products can still raise a bit of bile.

I also like it because from inside you really don't care. It's like walking into a fighty football supporters' pub in a suit of armour. There's a sense of 'and what are you going to do about it exactly'.

This really is a vast car. And, because the Laws of Automotive Styling say that the tyres must be exactly half the height of the car itself, they come up to my thigh. Then you have the radiator grille, which is bigger than my first flat, and the bonnet on which you could quite easily have a game of cricket. Certainly you could have a very major crash in a Phantom and simply not know.

There's also a sense of imperiousness, a sense that you really are driving round in Queen Victoria. It's the effortless power and the sense of empire. Yes, the leather may come from Bavarian cows, and all the components may arrive at the underground factory having already been assembled in Germany, but for all we know Elgar's quill was bought in Munich. It didn't stop his music from being as English as the Malvern Hills.

I loved my time with the Rolls as much as everyone else hated it, and me, for having one.

RIVA

It's not easy to decide which of man's creations is the most beautiful. It may be a painting, or a garden, or a building or perhaps one of Jordan's breasts.

Once, on a glorious summer's morning, I saw the Humber Bridge rising out of some dawn mist and thought it might well be the most beautiful thing I'd ever seen. But then there's the SR-71 spy plane and the Aston Martin DB7 and the Lamborghini Miura. The Guggenheim Museum in Bilbao isn't too shabby either.

However, after a long walk round the garden I've decided that the most jaw-dropping, eye-watering, hand-biting man-made spectacle of all time is the 1965 Riva Aquarama speedboat.

There's something about the angle of its prow and the positioning of that wraparound windscreen: it was actually based on the panoramic cinema screens that were popular at the time and this is the reason why the boat was called the 'Aquarama'.

Then you have the leatherwork in white and turquoise that seems to go so perfectly with the deeply polished mahogany hull, and the whole thing is finished off with a tail that tapers and flares just so.

Now, that the most beautiful man-made creation should have come from Italy is no surprise. There's a passion for aesthetics in Italy that you simply don't find anywhere else. But what about the most beautifully made creation? Is it the 1995 Honda Civic or maybe the Great Wall of China? Perhaps it's one of David Linley's wardrobes or a Brunel steamship? We shouldn't forget the Whitworth rifle either.

Well, I've just had another long walk round the garden and I've decided that the most perfectly crafted of all man's achievements, with the greatest attention to detail and quality, is, in fact, the 1965 Riva Aquarama. Oh, and it'll do 50 mph. All things considered then, quite a boat.

Riva began to make boats on the spectacular shores of Lake Iseo in northern Italy way back at the beginning of the nineteenth century. To begin with the products were simple, robust ferries really, but pretty quickly, this being Italy, they turned their attention to the notion of going quickly.

By 1934 they were going very quickly indeed. So quickly, in fact, that one of their 1500cc racers actually set a world speed record on water.

After the war things changed. Old man Riva, the third generation of the family that started it all, was keen to carry on making bash 'n' crash racers but his son, Carlo, had seen the new boats coming in from America and had other ideas. He wanted to make quality products for the leisure market.

There were furious rows over which direction the company should take. Some were so bad that Mrs Riva would have to step in and physically separate her brawling husband and son. And then one evening Carlo fell to his knees and said, 'Father, you can take that bottle from the table and hit me over the head with it. You can kill me, but I have to make my boats.'

Dad relented and Carlo was in business. At first he didn't appear to be very good at it. Fed up with the racing teams who argued that they must have a discount in exchange for all the publicity they brought, he doubled the price and scared them all away. Within weeks, then, he had no customers at all.

He also had no money, so he went to see the Beretta family who had made a fortune from guns. They gave him enough to buy six engines and off to America he went.

The first port of call was Detroit, where he had a meeting with the company that made the boats he so admired: Chris-Craft. They listened politely to the young man from Italy and said they'd be only too happy to supply him with engines providing he bought 50. That was 44 more than he could afford.

The next day he went back to see them and with a lot of shrugging said he'd love to buy 50 but sadly the post-war Italian government would only allow him to import six at a time. Very sorry. Nothing he could do. Hands are tied. The boys at Chris-Craft fell for the story hook, line and sinker and Carlo got his V8s.

Back at home he set about annoying as many customers as he could. Once, a German industrialist came to the factory and placed an order, then made the mistake of laughing when he was given the

The leatherwork in white and turquoise seems to go so perfectly with the deeply polished mahogany hull, and the whole thing is finished off with a tail that tapers and flares just so. Now, that the most beautiful man-made creation should have come from Italy is no surprise. There's a passion for aesthetics in Italy that you simply don't find anywhere else.

THE ITALIAN MOTOR INDUSTRY WAS USING 1.5 MICRONS OF CHROME ON ITS CARS. THE RIVA WAS USING 30 MICRONS.

delivery date. 'Don't be silly,' he said. 'There's no way you Italians could manage that.' Carlo threw him out.

He was completely obsessive. He colour-coded the staff's coats so the people in the woodyard wore red and the people in the engine bay wore yellow and so on. This way, if he looked out of his glass office and saw all the coats mingling, he'd know immediately that something was wrong.

Colleagues roll their eyes when they talk about the old days. 'I remember once,' said one, 'we spent all night going through pictures of our boats to see which was best for our publicity material. We didn't get finished until dawn, and then Carlo messed them all up again to see if we'd pick our original choices a second time around.'

Putting that much care into the pictures shows just how much care he put into the boats. He used the latest varnishes and varnished them again and again. And then again for good measure. The Italian motor industry was using 1.5 microns of chrome on its cars. He was using 30 microns on his boats. He was so pathological about quality that it was taking an age to get anything out of the factory and into the water. He reckoned on spending 1,500 hours to make one boat – a ludicrous amount of time for what was only an open pleasure craft – but pretty soon he was spending 3,000 hours on each one. Sometimes more.

Small wonder they became knows as the Rolls-Royce of boats, the Stradivarius of watercraft.

However, while his time and motion was a bit skew-whiff, his timing was impeccable because his crowning achievement, the Aquarama, came along in 1962. Which was pretty much the precise moment when the jet set really got into its stride.

In the olden days the idle rich played a bit of tennis and read a few books and that was about it. The only excitement came when someone decided to have a war. But then, towards the end of the fifties, they suddenly found that thanks to the jet engine and the helicopter they could pretty well go where they wanted, when they wanted. St Tropez for breakfast. St Moritz for lunch. St Albans for dinner even.

The epicentre of all this, the maypole in the playground if you like, was the South of France. And that meant they needed a boat, and because they were very rich they needed the best, and that meant that they all ended up at Carlo Riva's door.

Over the next few years the list of celebrity customers became a joke. He sold boats to Stewart Grainger, John Barry, Rex Harrison, Peter Sellers, Brigitte Bardot, Karl Heineken, Sophia Loren, Joan Collins, President Nasser, Victor Borge, King Hussein, Ferrucio Lamborghini, Prince Rainier, Roger Vadim and Richard Burton. The Aquarama became a mahogany passport to the high life.

Over in the States Chris-Craft were horrified and immediately stopped supplying engines, but this didn't stop Carlo. By then he was on such a roll he simply made his own. Beautifully, of course.

Eventually the boat-building world turned to glass fibre, which was tough and resilient, but Carlo refused to buckle. 'Here in Italy,' he told me once, 'we won't take a shit unless the lavatory seat is made from wood.'

His staff were equally vehement. One day, at Portofino, a Riva salesman was to be found berating some poor chap who'd dared to park his plastic gin palace in the harbour. 'Go away,' he shouted.

There's no power trim, no
adjustable this and active that.
You just get the wooden hull and
two V8s, but that's all you need.

IT TOOK 1,500 HOURS TO MAKE ONE BOAT – A LUDICROUS AMOUNT OF TIME FOR WHAT WAS ONLY AN OPEN PLEASURE CRAFT.

'Portofino is a beautiful place full of cultural heritage and only beautiful things can come here'.

It was no good though. The plastic boats started to take over and the Aquarama, at £250,000, started to look preposterously expensive. It soldiered on until 1996, by which time 3,760 had been made. But by then Carlo had sold the company to Vickers, who had introduced a glass-fibre cabin cruiser and were concentrating on restorations.

Horrified, he tried to buy the rights to his old boat back. But Vickers said no. Carlo told me it 'hurt his heart'.

Today you can buy one of his reclaimed Aquaramas for £250,000 – exactly the same as the damn thing cost new. But whatever, you will have one of the best-handling sports boats ever made. There's no power trim, no adjustable this and active that. You just get the wooden hull and two V8s, but that's all you need.

Gianni Agnelli, the playboy head of Fiat, once asked to try one out. He was told that if he could turn it over, he could have it. And Gianni, being Gianni, tried. But couldn't.

I tried too, one still morning on Lake Iseo. All I managed to do in one spectacular turn was hurl half a hundredweight of melted snow water into the cabin of the helicopter that was filming me. Quite what this tells us, I don't know. That I'm incompetent, or that the pilot was flying far too low – a bit of both probably.

What I do know is that of all the machines I've ever driven, flown or ridden the Aquarama remains my favourite, the one I'd most like to own. Yes, an F-15 fighter jet would be a laugh but I couldn't go anywhere in it, and yes, *Leander*, the superyacht, was spectacular but a bit of a bugger to run. Carlo's wooden baby, on the other hand, has a real-world attraction.

It hits all the bases too. It's fun, it's fast, it is exquisitely made and when you've finished looning around and you're back on dry land you can look back and think to yourself, 'That is the most beautiful thing I have ever seen.'

MILLENNIUM FALCON

When you're looking for the greatest spaceship ever made there are many choices, from *Discovery* in *2001: A Space Odyssey* to the *Liberator* from *Blake's Seven*.

But really, it comes down to a straight fight between the USS *Enterprise* from *Star Trek* and the *Millennium Falcon* from *Star Wars*.

So far as speed is concerned, well, that's a tough one. The *Enterprise* could tool along at warp nine, which appeared to be pretty fast. But is it faster than the *Falcon* in hyperdrive? It'd be interesting to ask Gene Roddenberry and George Lucas, the men who created these craft, to discuss it over tea and buns, but this isn't possible due to the fact that Mr Roddenberry is dead.

Obviously, with its photon torpedoes and its transporter room the *Enterprise* is by far the most sophisticated, but when it was destroyed in *Star Trek III* no one really shed a tear. They just built another. The *Millennium Falcon* could never be replaced.

Plus there was always a sense that it was the *Enterprise*'s captain and crew who won the day, *despite* the ship rather than *because* of it. I mean, the lumbering old barge was hopeless against a cloaked Klingon vessel. And even at full speed the Borg cube had no problem keeping up. Victory was only ever possible because of the ingenuity of Kirk and co.

In *Star Wars* it was the other way round. Han Solo and his trusty sidekick Chewbacca were always out of ideas and at the mercy of yet another death ray when, lo and behold, the *Falcon* would get them out of trouble. This made it as much of a character as R2-D2 or C-3PO.

But that said, Solo was a bit of a boy. I mean, when Picard encountered an asteroid belt he nosed through on a quarter impulse power. Han, on the other hand, just floored it.

And let's be honest, the *Falcon* was well tooled up. It had four turbo-lasers, a bunch of concussion-missile launchers and scanner-proof interior compartments for smuggling contraband. This, after all, is the purpose for which it was built.

It was won, in a game of cards, by Solo from his friend Lando Calrissian and then tweaked, customised and souped-up with a

THE *FALCON* WAS WELL TOOLED UP. IT HAD FOUR TURBO-LASERS, A BUNCH OF CONCUSSION-MISSILE LAUNCHERS AND SCANNER-PROOF INTERIOR COMPARTMENTS FOR SMUGGLING CONTRABAND.

double-power hyperdrive system. Unfortunately, much of the after-market accessories were fitted by Chewbacca, a Wookiee, who was modelled on the director's dog and speaks a language that's part walrus, part badger, part bear and part camel. Not the normal qualifications one needs for rocket science.

This probably explained why the *Falcon* was forever going wrong. Time and again Han and his rebel cohorts would have to bang the dashboard with their fists to get some wayward system working. And this too helped give the ship a flawed, almost human quality. This is something I look for in all machines . . .

Once upon a time I was in a country far, far away doing some filming for the television. The story called for us to join a band of ex-pats and Arabs on a motorised fun run through the desert outside Dubai, so obviously we needed some vehicles. Naturally, I went for a Range Rover, leaving the director with a Jeep Wrangler and the crew with a Discovery. The producer took a Mark One Toyota Land Cruiser pickup truck.

As the day progressed it quickly became apparent that a bunch of media types weren't exactly proficient in the art of desert driving.

The *Falcon* was forever going wrong. Time and again Han and his rebel cohorts would have to bang the dashboard with their fists to get some wayward system working. And this too helped give the ship a flawed, almost human quality. This is something I look for in all machines …

Those of us who had been 'off road' before had been taught to keep the revs as low as possible and use the engine's torque to pull us out of trouble. Slowly, slowly, gently, gently was the key.

Well, it may be the key in England, where the ground is wet and there are tree roots, but it sure as hell doesn't unlock any doors in the desert. Here if you let the engine's low-down grunt dribble you along, you sink into the soft sand and that's pretty much that.

What you have to do, I learned very quickly, is pretend you're in a stolen Astra on a housing estate at midnight. Keep it in as low a gear as possible, weld your right foot to the floor and drive like you're being chased by Darth Vader himself.

This doesn't work either because if you go too fast, you crest the lip of a dune, find a sheer drop on the other side and can't stop. So you slither down the slope and get bogged down in your own little avalanche on the other side. Or you rip a tyre off the rim. Or something important breaks. Either way, you end up as immobile as you would if you'd been crawling.

We made a sorry spectacle. The director going slowly because he had a bad back. The crew going slowly because the boot was full of delicate camera equipment and me going like a bat out of hell because it was fun. And all of us, ultimately, going nowhere.

All of us, that is, except the producer. His name is Andy Wilman and he is far from the best driver in the world. And yet, despite his fists of ham and his fingers of butter, he never got stuck once. This, we deduced, must have had something to do with his vehicle – the Land Cruiser pickup truck.

We were right. Even when it was up to its axles in powdery sand, that thing had enough grunt and enough traction to tow a bogged-down Range Rover. Nothing stopped it. No slope was too severe, no terrain too arduous. With its ancient diesel under the bonnet, its ladder chassis and its primitive four-wheel-drive system it was unstoppable.

It was, however, not pretty. I mean, the Mark One Land Cruiser pickup wasn't beautiful when it was new. After fifteen years of hard labour it was a sorry spectacle, its knobbly tyres bleached grey by the sun and its silver paintwork dulled, scratched and streaked with rust.

THE *MILLENNIUM FALCON* WAS STYLED TO RESEMBLE A BURGER. AND THE UNUSUAL, PROTRUDING CONTROL POD WAS MODELLED ON AN OLIVE THAT LUCAS SAW PEEPING OUT OF THE BUN.

Still, it was one of the best, most endearing and most lovable machines I've ever encountered.

We called it the *Millennium Falcon*.

The real *Falcon* was not beautiful either. When George Lucas was planning *Star Wars* he envisioned a sleek rocket, but his original design looked startlingly similar to craft being used at the time in the TV show *Space 1999*. So he went back to the drawing board, or rather the local burger restaurant.

It was here he got his inspiration. Yup, the *Millennium Falcon* was styled to resemble a burger. And the unusual, protruding control pod was modelled on an olive that Lucas saw peeping out of the bun.

The noise it made? Well, that was a recording of some experimental aircraft at the Oshkosh Air Show in 1976. And the battle scenes? Well, they were modelled on actual moves in the film *633 Squadron*. Especially the canyon-running in the final moments of *Star Wars IV*.

All of this helped create a sense of reality. But the icing on the cake was the model itself. Instead of being a titchy little thing on wires or a computer graphic it was real and it was big: five feet across and perfect in every detail.

That's the thing though. It was a model. This small detail, however, seems to have bypassed those who still live with their mothers and spend their evenings in the attic, reading magazines about murderers. These people have got it into their heads that the *Millennium Falcon* was real.

By analysing the film, frame by frame, they've worked out that it's 27 metres in diameter, with a thickness of 6.9 metres and a density of 4,000 cubic metres. Assuming that 95 per cent of this volume is air and the remaining material has the thickness of iron they have come up with the conclusion that it has exactly the same density as the USS *Enterprise*. Spooky.

One of them has even made this observation about the behaviour of the *Falcon* when it was hit by a burst of what, to you and me, is green light: 'The rotational kinetic energy of an object is 0.51^2 at non-relativistic rotational speeds. Therefore 3.902E8 joules of rotational kinetic energy were added to the *Millennium Falcon*. However, the physics of collisions involve conservation of linear or angular momentum rather than the conservation of kinetic energy, which only happens in elastic collisions.'

So, the green light has no mass. It is pure light energy. Interesting. And yet somehow not interesting at all.

Normal people didn't watch *Star Wars* as an endless series of freeze frames. Certainly I watched it in one lump and I thought it was terrific. All those space fights between creatures from worlds so much more strange than anything Captain Kirk had ever discovered.

This was the joy of *Star Wars*. It took us on a mind-bending flight of fancy and yet we swallowed all the nonsense because actually the tale itself was the old as the hills. You had the evil lord fighting the princess and her band of knights. And stuck in the middle was Han, the lovable rogue, with his pet monkey/dog and his amazing, beaten-up spaceship.

Small boys everywhere know that in a fight between Superman, James Bond and the Terminator, James Bond would win. Well it's the same story in *Star Wars*. In a fight between the *Enterprise*, *Stingray*, *Thunderbird 2* and the *Millennium Falcon*, the *Falcon* would reign supreme. It just would. The end.

SMALL BOYS EVERYWHERE KNOW THAT IN A FIGHT BETWEEN SUPERMAN, JAMES BOND AND THE TERMINATOR, JAMES BOND WOULD WIN. WELL IT'S THE SAME STORY IN STAR WARS. IN A FIGHT BETWEEN THE ENTERPRISE, STINGRAY, THUNDERBIRD 2 AND THE MILLENNIUM FALCON, THE FALCON WOULD REIGN SUPREME. IT JUST WOULD. THE END.

FLYING BOAT

It was 14 March 1939 and the Empire Flying Boat *Corsair* was already two days into its journey from Durban in South Africa to Southampton Water in England.

Nothing odd about that. This was a five-day journey back then because the plane would drop down several times a day for morning coffee, lunch and afternoon tea. Flying was civilised in those days.

But then, on the leg from Uganda to the Sudan, everything went horribly wrong. Pilot John Alcock, brother of the more famous Alcock who'd made the first ever flight across the Atlantic, put the plane on automatic pilot and went back to dispense some bonhomie among the passengers.

He returned to the cockpit just as the landing zone should have been coming into view. But it wasn't there. Assuming he'd overshot, he turned the plane around and retraced his steps but there was nothing below except jungle and swamp. After four hours of flying and with just fifteen minutes of fuel left in the tanks he knew he had to find the straightest piece of water he could and try to get *Corsair* and its thirteen passengers down safely.

The waterway he found was barely wider than the plane's wingspan but he made it anyway and had damn nearly brought the machine to a halt when the hull hit a partially submerged rock. With water gushing in, he applied full power and drove *Corsair* onto the beach.

No one was hurt and everyone was soon rescued and given shelter by a Belgian missionary who was quickly on the scene. Marvellous. End of story.

Except it wasn't. The *Corsair* was the most modern flying boat around in 1939, and her owners were determined that they weren't going to simply write her off and spend £50,000 on a new one. They decided that they would get her out.

The story is told beautifully in Graham Coster's book *Corsairville*, but, in summary, she was mended once but crashed on take-off. So they had to mend her again, even though the war was in full swing back at home. This involved damming the river and shipping in so many workers that a town had to be built. It's called Corsairville and it's still there today.

There is no doubt in my mind that this epic story, set against the background of war in Europe, would make a magnificent film. Having won the Battle of Britain single-handedly in *Pearl Harbor*, Ben Affleck would be the perfect quintessential Englishman, John Alcock. The Belgian missionary would be played by Jean-Claude Van Damme and his wife by Nicole Kidman. She gives good bodice.

Obviously, in the vast heat that is Africa, Nicole and Ben would fall madly in love. As he struggled to free the plane, she'd swoon at the muscles in his back writhing like a sack of pythons. He in turn would be mesmerised by her buttocks like ostrich eggs. Maybe Jean-Claude Van Damme could be eaten by a lion at some point.

However, no matter what happens or who they get to fill all the major roles, the star of the show would have to be the plane itself. The *Corsair*. Flying boats, you see, are just adorable. Partly this is because they were flying when flying was so glamorous, and partly it's because they were jacks of all trades but masters, if I'm honest, of none. They therefore have that most human of traits – a flaw.

The first thing you need to know is that they are flying boats with the emphasis on the word 'boats'. They are not to be confused with floatplanes, which are just normal aircraft that have flotation chambers instead of wheels. A flying boat really is a boat with wings; the underside of its fuselage really is a hull and as a result they are governed by all the usual maritime rules. They must, for instance, fly the flag of the nation onto whose waters they've landed.

When they first came along in the twenties they made perfect sense because airfields required all kinds of civil engineering and bulldozers, and it only took a brief shower to render them muddy and inoperable. In the twenties Heathrow and Gatwick were villages.

Whereas three-quarters of the world's surface was water and could therefore be used as a landing strip, either if something went wrong or when you reached journey's end.

America was the first nation to really get cracking with the notion of a plane that could take off and land on water. Spurred along by that great aviation pioneer Juan Trippe of Pan Am, they had three different models up and running before the rest of the world had even woken up.

THE NEW EMPIR

Two decks. **Smoking room.** **Promenade sa**
200 Miles an hour. **Now going**

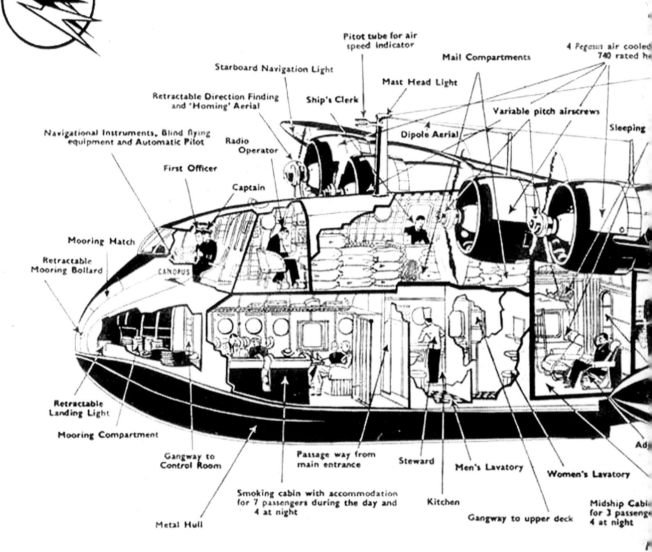

Pitot tube for air speed indicator

Starboard Navigation Light

Mail Compartments

Mast Head Light

Retractable Direction Finding and 'Homing' Aerial

Ship's Clerk

4 *Pegasus* air cooled 740 rated he

Navigational Instruments, Blind flying equipment and Automatic Pilot

Radio Operator

Dipole Aerial

Variable pitch airscrews

Sleeping

First Officer

Captain

Mooring Hatch

Retractable Mooring Bollard

CANOPUS

Retractable Landing Light

Mooring Compartment

Gangway to Control Room

Passage way from main entrance

Steward

Men's Lavatory

Women's Lavatory

Adj

Smoking cabin with accommodation for 7 passengers during the day and 4 at night

Kitchen

Gangway to upper deck

Midship Cab for 3 passenge 4 at night

Metal Hull

Length 88 ft.; Height from water line 24 ft.; Speed 200 mph (approx); Span 114 ft.; Weight fully

IMPERIAL

E FLYING-BOATS

on.   Sleeping berths.   3,000 Horse power.

to commission.   28 being built

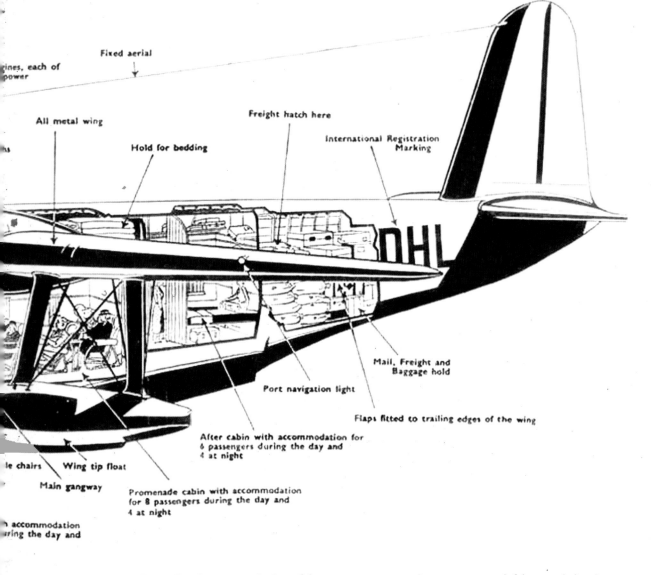

gines, each of
power

Fixed aerial

All metal wing

Hold for bedding

Freight hatch here

International Registration
Marking

Mail, Freight and
Baggage hold

Port navigation light

Flaps fitted to trailing edges of the wing

After cabin with accommodation for
6 passengers during the day and
4 at night

le chairs   Wing tip float

Main gangway

Promenade cabin with accommodation
for 8 passengers during the day and
4 at night

h accommodation
ring the day and

ded nearly 18 tons; Crew 5; Accommodation 24 passengers on day stages and 16 on night journeys

AIRWAYS

THE BOEING 314 HAD SEATING FOR 74 AND 36 BERTHS. THERE WAS A DINING ROOM, A DELUXE COMPARTMENT FOR VIPS, DRESSING ROOMS AND A LOUNGE.

They were called Clippers after the nineteenth-century sailing ships and they were all magnificent. The Boeing 314, for instance, had seating for 74 and 36 berths. There was a dining room, a deluxe compartment for VIPs, dressing rooms and a lounge. It made the *Orient Express* look like a Chinese ox cart.

And they were flown by just the most dashing people. Pilots were earning $8,000 a year at a time when a dentist could only make a quarter of that and a new Pontiac would cost just $500. This put the man in the hot seat on a par with the passengers, who were paying $500 dollars to be up there – the equivalent of £7,500 today.

Fine, but Britain wasn't simply going to sit by and let the vulgar, new-moneyed colonials have it all their own way. So a plan was hatched . . .

The Postmaster General announced in 1934 that all first-class mail would have to be carried by air. This provided an effective subsidy for any aircraft maker or airline who wished to invest in a long-haul carrier. So immediately Imperial Airways went in search of a plane that could cover the world. Shorts provided the answer with the Empire Flying Boat.

The were known as the C Class because all the names chosen – and *Corsair* was one of them – began with a C. They were lovely things, but sadly they were not quite so impressive as the American rivals. They could only carry 24 passengers and had a range of just 700 miles.

But that was enough to service the British Empire. And I'd like you to imagine that; flying to say Australia or India on one of these glorious machines in 1939, stopping every three hours or so in another country, in another time zone, for food and more tea. It must have been absolutely thrilling.

But the Americans by this stage were well ahead. Their planes were crossing the Pacific and then, on 26 March, they crossed the Atlantic too. We had a pit pony, charming and charismatic for sure, but they had a racehorse. In fact with the Sikorsky, the Boeing and the Catalina they had three racehorses and as a result they were on the brink of enveloping the world and bringing everyone a little closer together.

Sadly, it didn't turn out quite like that, because five months later Adolf Hitler sent his troops into Poland and the world fell apart.

In the build-up to war the British military had seen the advantage of flying boats and had already commissioned Shorts to build a version with guns instead of tea. It was called the Sunderland.

Like all the most human machines, the Deltic locomotive, the Space Shuttle and the Jumbo Jet, the windscreen rises up out of the nose to create more of a face. The Sunderland really did appear to have eyes and eyebrows and you know what, it even seemed to have an expression. It looked sad.

We had 40 by the time war broke out, each of which had a 7.7mm gun in the nose and two in the rear. In addition to this the Sunderland could carry 2,000 lbs of bombs, mines or depth charges. Small wonder the German U-boat crews used to call them 'flying porcupines'. They really did bristle with death.

Mind you, they weren't exactly fault free. In the early days bombs dropped at low altitude would sometimes bounce right off the water and hit the plane that had dropped them. And landing on water meant the pilot had to shift, in the blink of an eye, from being a master of the

The Sunderland became the most formidable anti-submarine weapon in the country's arsenal. In the five years of hostilities Sunderlands killed 28 U-boats and helped to destroy another seven.

air to being a salty sea dog with a nose for currents. Make no mistake, these things were not a walk in the park.

As the war rolled on the flying boat was given more powerful engines and eventually radar that became more and more sophisticated. Couple this to its ability to remain aloft for hour after hour and it became, despite the shortfalls, the most formidable anti-submarine weapon in the country's arsenal.

In the five years of hostilities Sunderlands killed 28 U-boats and helped to destroy another seven. To fight back the U-boats were given anti-aircraft guns, but it didn't do them much good. On one occasion they did manage to riddle a Sunderland so comprehensively that the crew on board knew they were finished. So they simply pointed the nose at the sub and deliberately crashed into it.

Eventually the battle of the Atlantic came down to a technological war between the radar in the planes and the radar-jamming equipment on the subs, a war Britain kept on winning.

But, surprisingly, the Sunderland was rather more than a flying listening station that could destroy targets when they were identified. It was also a damn good plane.

On 2 June 1943 a lone Sunderland was on patrol when it was jumped by no fewer than eight long-range Junkers Ju-88 fighters. Now even if the German pilots were blind and mad, a ratio of eight to one should have assured them of victory. I mean, apart from anything else, they were in fighters and they were up against a converted post-office van.

On their first pass the Sunderland was raked with fire and the forward machine gun was put out of action. On the second the radio was destroyed, and on each subsequent attack more damage was done. The crew didn't fare terribly well either. One was killed and the others suffered wounds of varying severity.

But on each of the passes the Germans were taking losses too, until only two of the original eight planes were left. They decided to scarper, leaving the wounded Sunderland to limp back to Cornwall where it landed safely and was driven on to the beach.

WE HAD 40 SUNDERLANDS BY THE TIME WAR BROKE OUT, EACH OF WHICH HAD A 7.7MM GUN IN THE NOSE AND TWO IN THE REAR. IN ADDITION TO THIS IT COULD CARRY 2,000 LBS OF BOMBS, MINES OR DEPTH CHARGES.

Eight to one. Not even a Spitfire could have managed that.

Unfortunately, however, while these flying boats were keeping the supply lines from America open their very future was being threatened back at home.

By the time the war ended Britain was a mass of airfields, which had been hastily built to house the vast numbers of fighters and bombers. So now there was no need to land at sea. Now new planes with wheels and jet engines could land six miles from the outskirts of London.

There have been attempts over the years to make jet-powered seaplanes. There was the Caspian Sea Monster, for one, and various attempts by the Americans. But really, everyone knew the flying boat was finished. Everyone, that is, except a company called Saunders Roe.

With airfields changing the face of air travel, this tiny Isle of Wight-based operation decided to have one last go at a truly magnificent flying boat. And what they had in mind wasn't that far short of sticking wings on a cross-channel ferry. What they had in mind was something called the Princess, a 105-seat monster.

It sounded daft but Saunders Roe had a reputation for thinking out of the box. Over time they built helicopters, rocket-assisted fighters,

The Princess had been taken out merely to see how she handled while taxiing but test pilot Geoffrey Tyson gave all ten engines some beans and up she went. Much later, when asked why he'd done this, he said, 'Well, she simply wanted to fly, so I let her.'

hovercraft and space probes, so when they said they were going to make a seaplane, when seaplanes were finished, and that theirs would have ten engines and six props and would weigh 320,000 lbs, the government said 'sure' and gave them £10 million.

It would be the biggest plane the world had ever seen, a 220-foot-wide double-decker fitted with all the appurtenances of gracious living. Powder rooms, restaurants. It would be Blenheim Palace in the air.

What staggers me about this project is that it didn't simply wither and die. The boffins at Saunders Roe really did get stuck in and make their amazing plane. And not just one but three of them. And then what staggers me even more is that on 21 August 1952 this giant did actually fly.

She had been taken out merely to see how she handled while taxiing but test pilot Geoffrey Tyson gave all ten engines some beans and up she went. Much later, when asked why he'd done this, he said, 'Well, she simply wanted to fly, so I let her.'

She actually flew on ten more test flights before someone somewhere realised she was heading in completely the wrong direction. The future of flight lay in low cost, not Earl Grey. Three or four hundred people crammed in like sardines, not 105 lounging around on sofas. And as a result the plug was pulled.

For years people wondered what might become of these three giants, which sat on the quayside on the Isle of Wight, rotting. At one point NASA showed an interest, thinking they could be used to transport Saturn V rockets. At another some bright spark suggested they could be used as a test bed for nuclear-powered aircraft. In the end, though, no one could think of anything and they were broken up for scrap.

I once saw a Princess and it left a lasting impression. Because unlike normal flying boats, which were planes with sculptured undercarriages, this one really did look like a giant boat, with a keel. And even allowing for the fact I was seven and small, it was absolutely bloody massive.

THE PRINCESS HAD TEN ENGINES AND SIX PROPS AND WEIGHED 320,000 LBS. IT WOULD BE THE BIGGEST PLANE THE WORLD HAD EVER SEEN.

It was also an example, like Concorde, of post-war Britain barking up the wrong tree and getting it wrong. However, when you encounter a magnificent folly in the grounds of a stately home, you often wonder what on earth possessed the old blue-blood to build such a thing. But you never think he shouldn't have bothered in the first place.

SS GREAT BRITAIN

In 1936 the governor of the Falkland Islands, Sir Henniker Heston, decided the old barge in Port Stanley harbour was really too far gone to be used as a floating coal and wool bunker any more. So it was towed out to the windswept and barren Sparrow Cove, where it was holed below the water line, beached and left to rot.

This was a sad day because the rusting old hulk wasn't a barge at all. It had started out in life as the SS *Great Britain*. The most amazing ocean liner of them all.

It wasn't the biggest or the fastest, and it certainly wasn't the most luxurious, but it was Genesis. A ship 50 years ahead of its time. The first iron-hulled steamship with a propeller ever to cross perhaps the most dangerous stretch of water in the world: the North Atlantic.

Of all the world's oceans this is the most psychopathic. The Southern Oceans are always angry and fierce. You know what to expect. But the North Atlantic can kill you in ways you never even thought possible. One moment it's calm and benign and then, just when you think the trip will be kind and friendly, you find yourself facing the kind of rogue wave that nailed George Clooney in *The Perfect Storm*. That's assuming, of course, you've managed to dodge the other shipping in the thick cloying fogs that hang over the Grand Banks for months on end, and to miss the icebergs that drift southwards from Greenland between June and September. But sometimes in other months as well, just to catch you out.

When we think of this 3,000-mile stretch of water we think of the *Titanic*, and we marvel at the loss of life. 1,500 souls going to their icy graves in what we assume was a freak accident. But it wasn't a freak at all. It was just another page in another chapter in a roll-call of death that boggles the mind.

History teaches us that in the eighteenth century France and Britain waged a war in America and that men, messages and supplies were routinely carried between the Old and New Worlds as though the crossing were some kind of train journey. Not so. In the 300 years after Columbus found the Americas tens of thousands died trying to follow in his footsteps. It is estimated that off the coast of Britain alone there

IN THE 300 YEARS AFTER COLUMBUS FOUND THE AMERICAS TENS OF THOUSANDS DIED TRYING TO FOLLOW IN HIS FOOTSTEPS. IT IS ESTIMATED THAT OFF THE COAST OF BRITAIN ALONE THERE ARE 250,000 SHIPS ON THE SEABED.

are 250,000 ships on the seabed, and in 1839 Parliament reckoned that 1,000 people a year were dying at sea.

Those that did make the journey talked of icebergs bigger than houses and massive waves over 100 feet tall. They spoke of 120mph winds and holes in the ocean. They spoke of a lumpen, vicious, white-flecked, freezing, grey, watery hell.

In the nineteenth century, engineering was beginning to work its magic. Invented as a concept in France, where bright men with huge foreheads sat around talking about the possibilities, it was taken up by the British, who actually dug the coal, made the iron and got the machines to work.

If anyone had come to Britain in, say, 1840, they simply wouldn't have believed their eyes. Elsewhere in the world it was sail and oxen, but here there were factories and steam engines and trains. It would have been like visiting a country today where they have interstellar travel and dogs in spacesuits. We were light years ahead.

Leading the charge was Isambard Kingdom Brunel. He'd cut his engineering teeth running a project to dig a tunnel under the Thames, the first tunnel ever to be excavated under water. Then he'd designed the Clifton Suspension Bridge and the Great Western Railway, or Mr Brunel's billiard table, as it became known.

Other engineers of the time were wary of putting their know-how to the test in a battle with the Atlantic. They had the machines to power ships but held back, fearful that no boiler, no matter how big and reliable, would be capable of dealing with such immense savagery. Investors held back too, fearful that their cash was bound to end up feeding the fishes.

What's more, there was a feeling that in order to have enough fuel to power the fires that heated the boiler all the available space on board would be taken up by coal. That meant no room for freight or passengers. And that rendered the whole idea pointless.

'Pah,' thought Brunel, and set to work. The idea, he told his paymasters at the Great Western Railway, was that you'd board a train at Paddington Station (which he also built), alight at Temple Meads in Bristol (yup, he built that too) and catch a steamship (which he would build) to New York from Bristol's floating harbour (which was also one of his).

The SS *Great Western*, a paddle steamer, was the result. There may have been only a handful of passengers on that first voyage but all were stunned with this new fangled device. 'She goes it like mad,' wrote one in his journal. 'Its motion is unlike that of any living thing I know; puffing like a porpoise, breasting the waves like a sea horse and at times skimming the surface like a bird.'

He made it sound terribly romantic, but actually it wasn't. Smoke from the funnel turned everyone's clothes black, cinders would regularly land in their hair, setting it alight, and the animal fats used as lubrication meant the whole ship smelled of bad cooking. Not good if you're seasick.

Still, the *Great Western* made the voyage in just fifteen days – the fastest ever crossing from England to America.

'Yesssss,' cried the world. Mankind has triumphed on land and now we have conquered the waves too. The age of the steamship is among us. We are invincible.

But we weren't. A company set up to rival Great Western built a ship called the *President*. Brunel thought it a lumbering mess and he was proved right, because it took a pathetic sixteen days to reach New York. On the way back things were even worse, because it simply never arrived. The ship, with 110 souls on board, just disappeared. Then there was the *Pacific*, which went missing with the loss of 186 lives.

This was a perennial problem back then and it had nothing to do with the Bermuda Triangle. There were no radios, no search-and-rescue helicopters and no radar. Ships had scheduled departure times, but because of the weather no one knew for sure when they'd arrive. Relatives waited and waited at quaysides, hoping to spot a telltale smudge of smoke on the horizon. Newspapers carried daily reports of vessels that had failed to dock. But nothing was ever heard of them again, and this meant no one knew just how terrifying it must have been to be aboard a liner that was going down in freezing seas, thousands of miles from land.

They got some idea, though, in 1854, when the steamship *Arctic* with 281 passengers on board – including many women and children – charged at full speed through a fog bank on the Grand Banks. She smashed head-on into a French steamer called the *Vesta*.

To begin with things went well. The chief engineer switched his pumps over to draw water from the bilges instead of the sea, thus turning the engine into an enormous pump. But it wasn't enormous enough and the ship began to go down by the nose. The crew threw the heavy anchor and chains overboard and the passengers were ordered to the back, to try to counterbalance the weight of the water.

Desperately, the crew tried to patch the holes in the wooden hull with mattresses and pillows but can you imagine that – using a pillow to keep the Atlantic Ocean at bay? Knowing his lifeboats could only take 40 of the 434 people on board, and thinking the *Vesta* would sink also, the captain ordered full steam ahead hoping to make land, which was 60 miles away.

Almost immediately the *Artic* ran over a lifeboat from the *Vesta*, killing all the occupants but one, and then all hell broke loose. Down

I'm surprised, frankly, that when the *Titanic* went down the world didn't simply shrug. 'Tch, there goes another one.'

Last Sunday's Count of Want Ads
Post-Dispatch.... 7149
Globe-Democrat, Republic, Star { All.... 6011
Post-Dispatch Gain over all four competitors 384

ST. LOUIS POST-DISPATCH

Only Evening Paper in St. Louis With the Associated Press News Service.

VOL. 64. NO. 240. ST. LOUIS, TUESDAY EVENING, APRIL 16, 1912—28 PAGES. PRICE ONE CENT

HOME EDITION

1302 LIVES LOST WHEN "TITANIC" SANK; 868 SAVED

Carpathia Steaming to New York With Survivors; None on Other Ships

NEW YORK, April 16.—Wireless from Capt. Roston of Carpathia, to Cunard line here, reads: "Proceeding to New York with about 800. Consulted with Mr. Ismay. So much ice about, considered New York best. Large number icebergs and twenty miles field-ice with bergs amongst."

MONTREAL, April 16.—The Allan Line issues the following statement: "We are in receipt of a Marconi via Cape Race, from Capt. Gambell of the Virginian, that he arrived on the scene of the disaster too late to be of service and is proceeding to Liverpool."

HALIFAX, N. S., April 16.—The Allan Liner Parisian reports by wireless, via Sable Island, that she has no passengers from the Titanic on board.

CAPE RACE, April 16.—Olympic reports by wireless "Carpathia reached Titanic position at daybreak FOUND BOATS AND WRECKAGE ONLY. Titanic sank about 2:20 a. m. in 41:16 n, 50:14w. ALL HER BOATS ACCOUNTED FOR, containing about 675 souls saved, crew and passengers included. Nearly all saved women and children. Californian remained searching exact position of disaster.

Giant Steamer Titanic as it would appear alongside the Eads Bridge; Ice bergs photographed off Newfoundland and St. Louis woman passenger rescued.

2-THIRDS WOMEN IN PARTIAL LIST OF THOSE RESCUED

Astor, Butt, Guggenheim and Many Other Famous Men Who Were on Board Not Mentioned Among Survivors---Money Loss Is $20,000,000.

By Associated Press.

ST. JOHNS, Newfoundland, April 16.—All hope that any of the passengers or any members of the crew of the Titanic other than those on the Carpathia are alive was abandoned here this afternoon. All of the steamers which have been cruising in the vicinity of the disaster have continued on their voyages.

HALIFAX, N. S., April 16.—The liner Parisian has reported by wireless that she steamed through much heavy field ice looking for passengers from the ill-fated Titanic. No life rafts or bodies were sighted among the floating wreckage which covered a large area. The Parisian reports that the weather was cold, and that even if any persons had been on the wreckage they would in all probability have perished from exposure before they could have been picked up.

NEW YORK, April 16.—There are among the 868 survivors of Titanic now on the Carpathia steaming for this port, 553 whose names have not been transmitted by the wireless. This gives hope to every friend of passengers of the ill-starred liner that the person they are interested in is one of the unnamed survivors. The mathematical chances are easily seen, as more than 1300 went down with the ship.

According to the best information obtainable, the death list is 1302. The total of passengers and crew is given at 2107 and 868 were saved. The White Star line has made the official announcement as to the number of survivors.

Of the 201 first cabin passengers thus far accounted for, 132 are women, 63 men and six children. Of the 114 second cabin passengers reported surviving, 88 are women, 16 men and 10 children.

It is known that Bruce Ismay, managing director of the White Star line was saved. John Jacob Astor, Maj. Archibald Butt, W. T. Stead, Jacques Futrelle, Washington Roebling, Henry B. Harris, Benjamin Guggenheim, Thornton Davidson and many other men noted in many fields were passengers and their fate is unknown. The chances are, considering the proportion lost and saved, that they went down with the ship.

The monetary loss probably will exceed $20,000,000. The magnificent ship cost about $10,000,000, cargo, mails and jewels were worth $10,000,000 more.

Besides the great financial loss incurred by the sinking of the Titanic with her cargo and passengers' property, the losses in accident insurance and life insurance resulting from the disaster will run into the millions.

P. A. S. Franklin, vice-president of the International Mercantile Marine Co. was asked if he could account in any way for the quick sinking of the Titanic, which he said repeatedly and confidently yesterday was an "unsinkable ship," and which represented all that modern marine engineering, architecture and unlimited financial backing could put into a transatlantic liner. He was asked, too if a lifeboat equipment of a capacity to carry only about one-third of the ship's company was in keeping with the advertised luxury and safety of the modern leviathans of the sea.

With bowed head and shaking voice, Franklin could find only this to say:

"Until the awful news came last night, I believed that even though two compartments of the Titanic were flooded, she would still float. The damage to her hull by the collision must have been beyond all imagination of the men who designed her. She must have been torn and ripped apart, as nobody ever believed a ship could be. We believed her boat equipment was adequate to meet any emergency. I cannot say more than that."

The brief wireless dispatches received so far show that passengers and crew passed through thrilling experiences from the very moment the Titanic crashed into the iceberg until the Car-

7 ST. LOUISANS ARE REPORTED SAFE ON BOARD CARPATHIA

Mrs. Robert, Misses Madill and Allen, Hays and Wife Rescued and "Silverthorne" Is on List.

ST. LOUISANS REPORTED SAFE

Mrs. Edward S. Robert.
Miss Georgette Madill.
Miss Elisabeth Allen.
Charles M. Hays.
Mrs. Charles M. Hays.
Mrs. Thornton Davidson.
"R. Spencer Silverthorne."
(Believed to be Spencer V. Silverthorne.)

Mrs. Thornton Davidson was Miss Orian Hays of St. Louis, the daughter of Mr. and Mrs. C. M. Hays. Mr. Davidson was on the Titanic also and the rescue of both has been reported. He is a well-known broker in Montreal.

Special to the Post-Dispatch.

MONTREAL, April 16.—A wireless message received here says that Charles M. Hays, president of the Grand Trunk Railway, is among the survivors aboard the Carpathia. His wife and daughter already had been reported saved.

In the incomplete lists of the rescued from the Titanic are the names of six St. Louisans and former St. Louisans who were among the first-class passengers. Relatives of all of them were notified by the Post-Dispatch Tuesday morning.

The lists contained the following names:

Mrs. Edward S. Robert, 4[illegible] Lindell boulevard.

Miss Georgette Madill, 4[illegible] Lindell boulevard.

Miss Elisabeth W. Allen, 4[illegible] Lindell boulevard.

Mrs. Charles M. Hays, now of Montreal.

Mr. and Mrs. Thornton Davidson, now of Montreal, and family.

"R. Spencer Silverthorne," believed to be Spencer V. Silverthorne, [illegible] Von Versen avenue.

Survivors Aboard Carpathia.

All of these, according to wireless messages, were taken aboard the Carpathia. There is some question as to the identity of Silverthorne, but his relatives believe the St. Louisan was rescued. They had been advised by him that he was to sail on the Titanic.

Relatives of Mr. and Mrs. Charles M. Hays were greatly concerned over the fate of the husbands of Mrs. Hays and her daughter, Mrs. Thornton Davidson. The wire to the Post-Dispatch from Halifax saying that Hays was among the rescued greatly reassured them, although there was still no news from Davidson.

Members of the family were puzzled over the name of Miss Margaret Hays in the list of survivors. Marjory Hays was the maiden name of Mrs. George Hall, a daughter of Mr. and Mrs. Hays, who is with her husband in Boston. Mrs. Davidson formerly was Miss Orian Hays of St. Louis.

Mrs. Hays is the sister of Norris B. Gregg of the Buckingham Hotel, William H. Gregg, [illegible] Laclede avenue, and Mrs. L. Kotany, [illegible] Laclede avenue.

Charles M. Hays is president of the Grand Trunk Railway, with offices in Montreal. He was formerly general manager of the Wabash with headquarters in St. Louis and has a wide acquaintance here. He is a son of former Postmaster Hays of St. Louis. Davidson is a broker.

Papin Said to Be in Rome.

St. Louis relatives of Theophile Papin Jr., who was supposed to have been aboard the Titanic, received, at noon Tuesday, a telegram from his sister, Mrs. Gerald Borden of New York City, announcing that she had received a cablegram from Papin at Rome. Mrs. Borden formerly was Miss Lucille Papin of St. Louis.

The Papin & Tontrup Realty Co., of which Papin is a member, said they sent a cablegram to Papin at Rome Tuesday morning but had received no reply.

George W. Allen, [illegible] Cabanne avenue, father of Miss Elisabeth Allen, said he was overjoyed to hear that she and the others in her party, her aunt, Mrs. Robert, and her cousin, Miss Madill, were safe.

Thornton Davidson and Family Reported Safe.

MONTREAL, Canada, April 16.—Piers Davidson, brother of Thornton Davidson, received a wireless message from Newfoundland saying Thornton Davidson and his family had been saved.

FLOATING ICE OFF NEW FOUNDLAND

STERN VIEW of THE TITANIC....

Miss ELISABETH W. ALLEN...

ABOUT 2200 PERSONS WERE ABOARD TITANIC.

Passengers of all classes	1310
Crew	[illegible]
Women and children in first cabin	140
Women and children in second cabin	97

White Star line officials say that a small number of passengers may have been taken on after the booking list was made up, and that the crew may be a little larger or smaller than stated.

Lifeboats for Only One-Third on Board

NEW YORK, April 16.

THE Bureau of Inspection of Steam Vessels gives statistics of the life-saving apparatus of the Olympic, the Titanic's sister ship. As the two ships are almost identical in size and capacity, it is not likely that their life-saving equipment differs materially.

The Olympic has 16 lifeboats and four collapsible boats, or rafts, calculated to accommodate [illegible] persons. This means about one-third of the total number of passengers and crew together, which is [illegible]. The Olympic carries [illegible] life-preservers and [illegible] life-buoys.

TITANIC IS BURIED 2 MILES UNDER WATER

HALIFAX, N. S., April 16.

THE death bed of the [illegible] steamer Titanic and of many who must have been dragged with her, is two miles, at least, below the surface of the sea.

The calculation was made by an official of the Government Marine Department, who finds that depth on the marine chart at a point about [illegible] miles from Halifax and about [illegible] miles south of the Grand Banks, where he believes the Titanic went down.

This location is about midway between Sable Island and Cape Race and in line with that dangerous place, which, however, might have proved a place of safety had there been time to run the Titanic there and beach her.

7,000,000 PIECES OF MAIL ON STEAMER

NEW YORK, April 16.

POSTMASTER EDWARD M. MORGAN stated today that the White Star liner Titanic had on board [illegible] sacks of mails. It is not likely, he said, that the mails were saved. As the standard ocean mail bag holds about [illegible] letters it is estimated that in all about 7,000,000 pieces of mail matter have been lost.

GOVERNMENT TO MAKE INVESTIGATION

WASHINGTON, April 16.—A quick report from the White Line on the number of lifeboats and life rafts carried by the Titanic has been telegraphed for by Supervising Inspector Uhler of the Government Steamboat Inspection Service.

MISS QUIMBY FLIES ACROSS THE CHANNEL

BOULOGNE-SUR-MER, France, April 16.—Miss Harriet Quimby, American airwoman, crossed the English Channel from Dover this morning, landing at Hardelot, near this port.

Miss Quimby is the first woman to fly across the channel alone. Her flight occupied two hours.

JACK KNEW!

This is the paper that printed the ad that rented the house that Jack built.

MARCH COUNT

Of House, Flat and Business Property For Rent Wants.

POST-DISPATCH 3425
All of the Four Competitors Combined 3263

St. Louis' ONE BIG Newspaper

WEDNESDAY FAIR, SOMEWHAT WARMER

THE TEMPERATURES.

3 a. m.	38	7 a. m.	42
5 a. m.	40	9 a. m.	[illegible]

Yesterday's Temperatures.
High, 79 at 4 p. m. Low, 58 at 5 a. m.

Clouds are the bill the weather forecaster holds out for St. Louis Tuesday evening. A few light showers may come.

If the forecast is correct the skies will clear Wednesday and slightly higher temperatures will be recorded in the afternoon.

St. Louis, in spite of the cool wave that came Monday night, is fortunate in comparison with some sections of the country. The mercury fell to 28 degrees in Western Nebraska and the Dakotas, and killing frosts were reported from various areas.

Heavy rains have been drenching Arkansas and the states along the Gulf of Mexico.

Official forecast for St. Louis and vicinity: Cloudy weather tonight; Wednesday fair, somewhat warmer Wednesday afternoon.

CARPATHIA DUE THURSDAY NIGHT

Vessel With Survivors May Be Reached From Sable Island.

NEW YORK, April 16.—Intense interest centers in the gradual approach to New York of the Liner Carpathia, bearing the 868 survivors of the Titanic. It is this ship which promises to bring the first authentic details of the great tragedy and the scenes that followed. The Carpathia is a slow vessel, and is due at Sandy Hook about 11 o'clock Thursday night.

Meanwhile the Carpathia will be within the wireless range of several stations along her course. Her wireless plant has a radius of about 150 miles, according to the Cunard company. She will be south and abreast of Sable Island late today or tomorrow at a distance of about 125 miles and may come within direct wireless communication with Sable Island. Her present communication is by wireless relay to the Olympic and other intervening ships having a greater radius of wireless.

in the bowels of the ship the stokers and engineers could see perfectly
well that this race for the shore was a battle they were going to lose.
They could see how fast the water was rising and downed tools.

Now we've all seen *Titanic*, in which the crew kept order as women
and children were loaded into the lifeboats. It wasn't like that on the
Arctic. The crew, an angry knife-wielding mob, went berserk, charging
onto the deck and refusing to obey the captain's orders. The chief
engineer, with nine of his men, seized one lifeboat and made off with
food, water and cigars. It was every man for himself and only the fittest
would survive. People were making rafts out of anything they could
find, but before they were finished the rafts were stolen by the mob.

Of the 153 crew on board 61 were rescued, including the captain.
But only 23 of the 231 passengers came out of the ordeal alive.

As news of the disaster spread people were horrified at the
extraordinary antics of the crew and the appalling loss of life.
Suddenly everyone had documentary proof that death on a sinking
ship was one of the worst imaginable. The panic and the sense of
total desperation. The knowledge that you and your children were
going to die, painfully, and that there was absolutely nothing you
could do about it. And then came the *Atlantic*.

The *Atlantic* was a stunning ship, but unfortunately her captain
was a stunning drunk. He thought he had enough coal on board for
the outbound voyage, but sadly it wasn't South Wales coal, which
burned well and slowly. The Welsh were on strike at the time, so
instead he'd loaded up with fast-burning Lancashire coal. As the
mighty ship approached the fearsome Grand Banks the chief
engineer announced that they might run out.

The captain didn't want to be late to New York so he ordered
the engines up to full speed, reckoning he could make Halifax,
refuel and still be on time in the Big Apple.

Unfortunately he didn't really know where he was, and he
wasn't prepared to stop and take soundings. And so he was probably
as surprised as anyone when, on a completely clear night, he hit
Canada doing twelve knots.

This was right at the height of mass European emigration to America. And as a result there were 1,000 people on board.

Within six minutes the ship had pretty much sunk and many had taken to the masts, where they clung, being battered by the freezing winds and even more freezing waves. Some of the crew reckoned they could make land and attempted to get a line to a rock 40 yards away. They managed it, and 200 people crawled to what they thought was safety.

But so severe was the weather that only a handful ever got from the rock to the shore. The rest simply froze to death before local fishermen were able to row out in the morning. It's estimated that 585 people were killed that night and, as with the *Arctic* disaster, the crew fared much better than the passengers – 94 of the 146 on board survived.

Then you have the *City of Glasgow*. Unusually, it caught fire, incinerating most of the lifeboats before they could be launched. And some of those that were winched to the sea were chopped to pieces by the still spinning prop. The death toll from that one was 471.

I'm surprised, frankly, that when the *Titanic* went down the world didn't simply shrug. 'Tch, there goes another one.'

Maybe the accident became etched on the national consciousness because, for once, the crew behaved like gentlemen and didn't trample on women's heads to get to the lifeboats. Or maybe it's because the *Titanic* had been described as being unsinkable. Or maybe it's because the ship was on its maiden voyage. Or perhaps it had something to do with the sheer numbers. I mean, 1,200 dead, that's phenomenal.

I think, though, the main reason why the *Titanic* disaster is remembered, while most of the others aren't, is that it went down in the twentieth century. And by then ocean travel had changed from being a hazardous and uncomfortable experience into the single most luxurious event in a man's life.

At the beginning of the steamship era there were three distinct ways of getting across the Atlantic. You had the ultra-luxurious American

The 10,500-horsepower *Mauretania* set a transatlantic record in 1902 and it wasn't beaten for another 22 years. The *Mauretania* was not only fast and vast but also beautiful. Imagine the Palace of Versailles at sea, then double the size and double the luxury and you're still not halfway there.

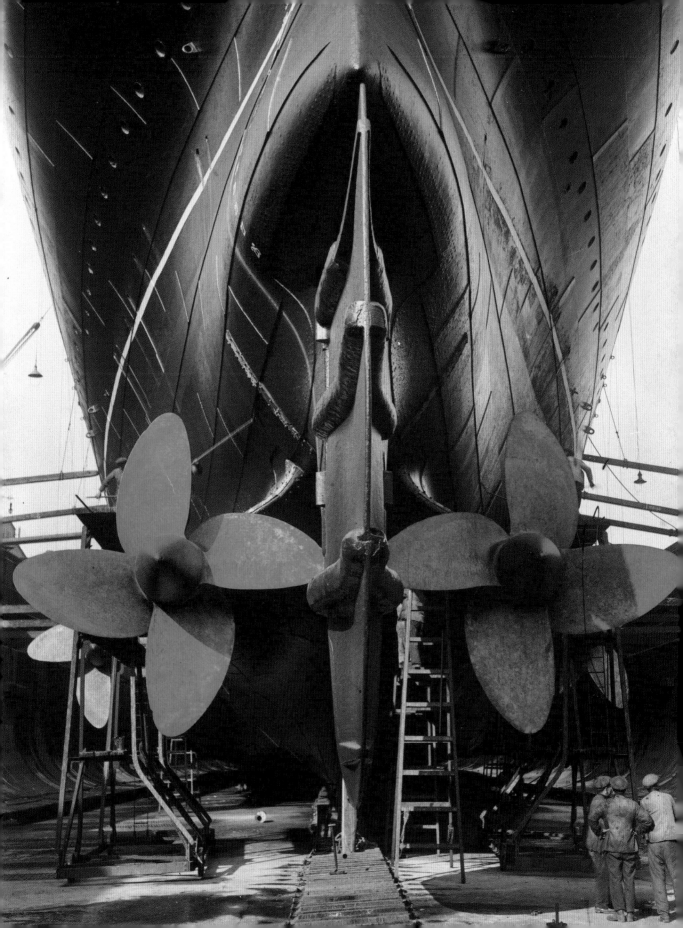

ships from the Collins line, and the cheap and cheerful ships for immigrants from the Inman line. In between there was Cunard, who were only interested in being sensible. It is remarkable that in the torrent of death that befell ocean travel in the late nineteenth and early twentieth centuries Cunard didn't lose a single passenger.

And they can hardly be blamed for their first casualties in 1915. Because it wasn't carelessness that killed them, or bad management. It was a German torpedo that slammed into their ship, the *Lusitania*; 1,201 died.

As time wore on other steamship operators came along and as a result the oceans turned into a racetrack where civic and national pride were at stake. Every ship that slithered down its ramps, dripping champagne, had to be faster and more luxurious than the one that went before. The Germans had to beat the Americans. The French had to beat the British. And the British, led by Cunard, had to beat everyone.

Although the companies that operated these leviathans would never admit to racing one another – they didn't want the public to think they were being reckless – there is no doubt that liners did line up for full-bore crossings, often racing at full pelt side by side for days on end.

On deck passengers would bet on which ship would win and shout insults if theirs started to pull ahead. There was a particularly epic duel between the *City of New York* and the *Teutonic* with both ships crossing the line in New York, after a 3,000-mile race, just nine minutes apart.

This rivalry and racing ended, however, with Cunard's *Mauretania*. Sister to the *Lusitania*, it was 600 feet long, fitted with four propellers and could carry 2,165 passengers at speeds that simply blew everything else into the middle of last week. She could average, on a normal crossing of the Atlantic, an incredible 25 knots.

Do not think that the *Titanic* was trying for a record when it ploughed into that iceberg because, quite simply, it wouldn't have stood a chance. The 10,500-horsepower *Mauretania* set a transatlantic record in 1902 and it wasn't beaten for another 22 years.

The White Star Line's *Titanic* was only trying to prove it wasn't *that* slow when it hit the berg and proved it wasn't *that* well designed either.

The *Mauretania* was not only fast and vast, and not only built with Cunard's eye for detail, but also beautiful. And more than this, she was kitted out in a blizzard of grace and panache. There were Adam fireplaces and wood panelling with bronze and crystal chandeliers. There were references to Louis XVI and the first-class cabins were littered with the finest Georgian furniture. In the main lounge fluted mahogany columns supported the beamed ceiling, and on the floor only the finest silk carpets would do. Imagine the Palace of Versailles at sea, then double the size and double the luxury and you're still not halfway there.

There was technology too, and not just in the engine room. The lavatories, for instance, had door-operated valves, so they flushed every time someone entered or left the room. The lifts, to save weight, were made from a new type of metal called aluminium. There was even a fully equipped hospital.

It was the *Mauretania* that set the tone for the liners that flew across the Atlantic in the post-war years. The *Normandie*, the *France*, the *United States* and the *Queen Mary*. You could even argue that the *Mauretania* gave rise to the cruise ships that ply the Med and the Caribbean today. Yes, plastic has replaced the wood panelling and turbines have replaced the boilers, but the idea is still the same. The last word in luxury. The best food. The quietest engines. And the greatest possible speed.

Today the *Mauretania* is long gone, although her luxurious innards were rescued and now line the bar area of a nightclub in Bristol.

Some say the Cunard flagship was just the greatest liner ever but, not wishing to be cussed, I'm not so sure. I think that accolade rests with Brunel's follow-up to the *Great Western*. The SS *Great Britain*.

In its day the wooden *Great Western* had been something of a success, and its owners asked Brunel for a sister ship. Naturally, they thought it would be pretty much the same. Maybe the coal stores could be moved from the stem and the stern to somewhere nearer the

The *Mauretania* set the tone for the liners that flew across the Atlantic in the post-war years. The *Normandie*, the *France*, the *United States* and the *Queen Mary*. You could even argue that the *Mauretania* gave rise to the cruise ships that ply the Med and the Caribbean today.

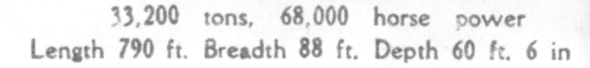

33,200 tons, 68,000 horse power
Length 790 ft. Breadth 88 ft. Depth 60 ft. 6 in

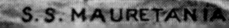

S. S. MAURETANIA.

THE *GREAT BRITAIN* WAS 50 PER CENT LONGER AND THREE TIMES ROOMIER THAN THE WOODEN CUNARD RIVALS. IT WAS BY FAR AND AWAY THE BIGGEST MAN-MADE MOVING OBJECT THE WORLD HAD EVER SEEN.

boilers, and maybe something could be done about the roll that made passengers so sick. But broadly, they didn't want to deviate too much from what was a well-proven vessel.

They were reckoning without the ambition of Isambard Kingdom Brunel. Wood, he figured, was completely wrong for what was actually a machine. Steam trains were not made from elm and nor were the tracks fashioned from oak. So, he decided that his new ship would have an iron hull.

Then, when work was well underway, he saw a propeller-driven boat put-putting around Bristol harbour and thought, 'Hang on a minute; if a prop can work in coastal waters, why can't it work in the ocean?' So, much to his paymasters' despair, he threw away the designs for the paddle wheels and started again with a screw.

He'd been the first with ocean-going steam power. Now he was going to be first with a continent-hopping iron hull and first with a prop. No ship had even been the subject of such intense scrutiny. Every nut and bolt was pored over by the press and Prince Albert came to the launching ceremony, where he spent two hours touring the innards, scarcely able to believe his eyes.

In wooden ships of the time the beams and the supports were great chunks of oak. But in the *Great Britain* there were slender beams of iron. You only have to look at the roof of Paddington Station to see how delicate Brunel could be. But then you only had to look at the propeller shaft to see he could play heavy metal with the best of them. It was 130 feet long and weighed a whopping 36 tons.

And it wasn't just the technology that impressed; it was the sheer size. This thing was 50 per cent longer and three times roomier than the wooden Cunard rivals. It was by far and away the biggest man-made moving object the world had ever seen.

Brunel's rivals were surprisingly joyful as the ship took shape in Bristol, because they felt the diminutive wonderbrain had bitten off more than he could chew with this one. With barely contained glee they waited for the whole project to be a disaster. And they didn't have to wait long.

First of all, with a cruising speed of nine knots, she turned out to be slower than Cunard's wooden paddle steamers, and because there were no paddle boxes on either side she did roll badly in heavy seas. Nothing could be done about this, but alterations were made to her prop in a bid to increase the speed. Obviously they weren't a success, because on her second trip to the States three blades simply fell off.

It was repaired in America, but on the return leg it fell to pieces again. And so she arrived in Liverpool, after a miserably slow twenty-day crossing, under sail. By this stage the season was over, so she was laid up for the winter, a technical and financial failure.

In those dark, cold days Brunel toiled with the prop, spending more and more money on new designs, and desperately tried to think of ways to stop the disconcerting roll. But the tide of public opinion was turning against him. One magazine, which had loved the ship when it was being built, said it was 'leviathanism which was wholly uncalled for'. Some even questioned Brunel's engineering ability. Yeah right. What did they expect? That you could just pop a brand-new idea into the water and off it would go.

The *Great Britain* limped into the Falkland Islands, where she was turned into a floating wool and coal bunker until she became so riddled with holes they took her round to Sparrow Cove and left her to die.

The fact is that in 1842 Brunel had seen the future. He knew that props and vast iron hulls were the way forward and as usual he was right. Given time, there's no doubt he could have made the *Great Britain* work. But time was running out.

In only its second season, for some extraordinary reason, the captain failed to find the Atlantic and crashed into Ireland. No one was hurt but the ship was stuck fast and so, with winter closing in, her owners decided that was that.

Brunel was incandescent with rage. He went to the crash site and found his ship, virtually undamaged, on the beach. 'It is positively cruel,' he wrote. 'It would be like taking away the character of a young woman without any grounds whatever.'

Back in London he set about the Great Western steamship company, using his second-greatest skill. As a bright and educated man, he could cajole and bully and sweet-talk anything out of anyone. He'd forced his bosses to cough up the vast sum of £117,000 to build the *Great Britain* and then, just as the shareholders were staging a revolt over the cost, he talked them out of another £53,000 for her dock in Bristol. Now he needed £34,000 to rescue her from the beach.

It would be, everyone knew, a waste of money. The ship could never, in a thousand years, repay the debt. It was a lost cause. Everyone with a hint of financial know-how could see it was better to let her rot. But Brunel talked them into it nevertheless. He got his ship back to sea and in doing so finished the company.

As it turned out the *Great Britain* never did make a success of the transatlantic route, and rather than try to improve her Brunel had moved on and was busy killing himself with the *Great Eastern*, a ship so enormous it could steam to Australia without refuelling.

In the end the *Great Britain* was sold for £25,000, after just eight trips to America, and spent the next 40 years plying the world's oceans, mostly under sail. She was used as a troopship both in the Crimean War and during the Indian Mutiny and then one day, in 1886, when she was taking coal from South Wales to San Francisco, she was caught in a storm off Cape Horn and virtually wrecked.

She limped into the Falkland Islands, where she was turned into a floating wool and coal bunker until she became so riddled with holes they took her round to Sparrow Cove and left her to die.

Happily, in the 1970s an American benefactor sent a pontoon to the Falklands, wrapped the old girl up in bandages and brought her back to Bristol, where she sits now, restored and resplendent and waiting to greet visitors.

A failed ship? A flaw in Brunel's armoury? Some say so. Some say he was out of his depth and had no understanding of the sea. But come on. Imagine what the Americans must have thought when this astonishing iron monster chugged into New York with no visible means of propulsion. The sails were down, there were no paddle wheels. But she was moving. And imagine their surprise as they moved closer and found that she was made from iron.

The SS *Great Britain* was the biggest hammer blow to American pride until Concorde touched down at JFK nearly 150 years later. They'd beaten us in the War of Independence, but when they saw that ship they must have wondered how. Doesn't that make you feel a little bit proud?

Yes, I agree, it didn't work. And many would say lots of Brunel's ideas were similarly flawed. They point at the atmospheric railway he built in Devon, saying it was ridiculous to use a vacuum pump to suck trains along a track. And they reminisce with titters about his broad-gauge railway.

But think about it. With the atmospheric system, Brunel had taken the power source off the engine and put it in a pumping station. In much the same way that modern electric locomotives take their oomph from a power station. And everyone agrees that if the country had stuck with his idea for a seven-foot gap between the tracks, instead of the 4' 8" we have now, it'd be much easier to design trains that could corner at 200 mph or more.

Brunel's problem was that he was thinking twenty-first-century thoughts in a nineteenth-century world.

That showed on his ships. Yes, the *Mauretania* set the tone for modern cruise liners. But the *Great Britain* set the scene.

ARTHUR

Thirty years ago the weather forecast may as well have been written by J. K. Rowling. Every night we were served up another dose of fiction and nonsense, none of which had anything to do with what the weather would actually be like the next day.

But in recent years you may have noticed that things have changed. When they say it'll be wet it usually is wet. They can see a cold snap coming a week before it gets here. And they can predict where the winds will be strong enough to down chimney pots and where they won't. Some of this new-found ability is down to much better computers, but mostly it's due to the satellite.

And it's not just weather forecasting that has benefited from these space-based messenger boys. In fact, when you stop and think about it, vast chunks of modern life are reliant on them as well. Without those eyes in the sky cars, planes and boats would have to rely on human guidance. Which means 747s bound for Heathrow would end up at South Mimms services. Furthermore, we would never be able to see live sporting events from the other side of the world. International calls on your mobile would be impossible. America wouldn't be able to keep its eye on developments in the Middle East. And, most important of all, you wouldn't be able to stay up half the night watching Jo Guest frolicking naked on the sun-drenched island of Jamaica.

To quench our seemingly insatiable thirst for better communication and more TV, the vast emptiness of the universe isn't empty any more. There are, in fact, 9,000 satellites orbiting earth, and the business of getting them there has turned space into a dustbin. Insurance specialists say there are probably 100,000 pieces of space debris too small to catalogue and tens of millions of man-made particles.

This is beginning to make space travel in the vicinity of earth extremely hazardous. The Shuttle recently hit a paint chip, which doesn't sound like the end of the world, but because of the speeds involved the tiny particle blew a hole halfway through one of its windows. More recently the French-made satellite *Cerise* was destroyed when it crashed into a piece of debris.

Then there's the bothersome business of all this rubbish

coming back down to earth. It's estimated that in 1999 nearly half a million pounds of junk re-entered the atmosphere. 84,000 lbs survived the heat and, because 25 per cent of the earth's surface is land, we can deduce that 21,000 lbs didn't fall harmlessly into the sea.

In the eighties the Canadians had a bust-up with the Russians over large chunks of radioactive space waste that landed in the Northern Wilderness. And the Australian government charged NASA with littering after *Skylab* crash-landed in the outback.

It's all a far cry from the system of space communication dreamed up by the then-unknown science-fiction author Arthur C. Clarke. Back in 1945, in a paper called 'Extra-Terrestrial Relays', he suggested that three satellites positioned 22,000 miles from earth would mean the whole planet could be linked.

It was a wonderful piece of speculation, especially since there was no way, back then, of reaching even five feet into space. Rocketry was limited to a handful of British geeks, who understood it only in theory, and the Nazi V2s, which had a job reaching England, leave alone the heavens.

So how Clarke thought his satellites could be taken to their carefully chosen mooring spots 22,000 miles away, God only knows.

Actually, that's not true. Today it isn't only God that knows. Anyone with access to the internet can find out as well. The thing is, though, it's a bit complicated. It really is rocket science.

You see, in order to break free of the earth's atmosphere you need to achieve a speed of 8 km per second. That's 17,500 mph. And that's pretty fast.

At this speed your forward momentum exactly balances the downward gravitational acceleration so you achieve orbit. Fine, but it will be a low orbit, just a few miles up, and you will still be battling traces of friction from the atmosphere. In time, a few months maybe, your expensive satellite will start to slow down, and when that happens the people on earth had better stay indoors because it's going to starting raining steel . . .

What you need is a huge rocket capable of getting you up to 17,500 mph and then, when you're cruising round the world, another rocket to take you far, far away.

22,000 miles, as Clarke predicted, is perfect because here the satellite has a huge view of earth – it can therefore beam its pictures or information to a wide area – and what's more, for mathematical and scientific reasons I simply don't understand, its speed can be perfectly matched to the rotation of the earth. Think. The dish that brings Jo Guest into your sitting room is pointing at a satellite that's howling through space at thousands of miles per hour, but from your point of view on earth it's always in the same place.

This is handy. Imagine how annoying it would be if Jo were just about to remove her top when the satellite moved. You'd have to go outside with a ladder to wave your dish about until you found it again.

Of course, pumping geo-stationary satellites into space today is a piece of cake. Even the French can do it. But back in the early days it wasn't even remotely possible.

The Russians were the first to get up there with *Sputnik*. It was little more than a radio beacon, screaming round the world beeping.

The Americans were next. A huge mirror called *Echo* was sent up there, just getting out of the atmosphere where it reflected radio signals back to earth.

The first proper satellite that could receive a signal, amplify it and then send it back to the other side of the earth was launched on 10 July 1962. It was called *Telstar*, and the Queen, in her Christmas message that year, called it 'the invisible focus of a million eyes'.

It was a remarkable advance for humankind. A true triumph. Because it was high enough to see America and Europe at the same time events in New York could be beamed, live through space, to sitting rooms in Britain and France.

Well, that was the theory. But *Telstar* did not sit at the same place over the earth. The Delta rocket that took it into space was simply not powerful enough for that, so it rose and set like the moon, the sun and all the other stars . . . only a lot faster. It would only be visible from Britain for 40 minutes and then you had to wait two and a half hours for it to go all the way round the world and come back again.

You needed to hope, then, that the sporting event it was capturing as it flew over America didn't go into extra time.

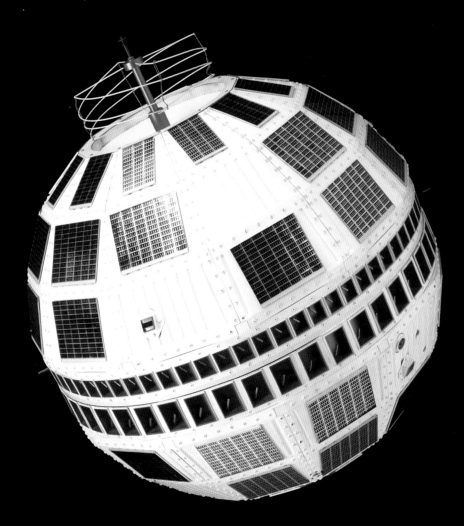

The first proper satellite
that could receive a signal,
amplify it and then send it
back to the other side of the
earth was launched on 10
July 1962. It was called
Telstar, and the Queen, in her
Christmas message that
year, called it 'the invisible
focus of a million eyes'.

Arthur was the first open satellite dish in the world and he was a leviathan. But of course he had to be 30 metres in diameter if he was to stand a chance of pinpointing that pinprick in the sky. He also had to be fast, and he was. He may have weighed 1,180 tons but he could turn a complete circle in three minutes while moving from the horizontal through 90 degrees to the vertical. What on earth people must have thought when he was unveiled? This huge white saucer, supported on a latticework of girders, tracking an invisible object in the sky so we in Britain could see what was going on in America . . . right now. He must have seemed like science fiction.

And that was just the start of the problems. The really big one was trying to track and lock on to what was nothing more than an electronic beach ball that was 2,000 miles away, doing 14,000 mph.

Britain took up the challenge, and just before *Telstar* was launched opened a ground station at a place called Goonhilly on the Lizard Point in Cornwall. The Lizard was ideal, partly because it's as far south as you can go in Britain, which eked out the maximum time *Telstar* would be visible, but also because the rock down there is super-stable. Any tremor, any movement at all, and the whole project would be dead in the water.

Nevertheless, the ground station worked. *Telstar* worked. And on 11 July 1962 Britain heard Alistair Cooke live, via the heavens, from New York. Just seventeen years after Arthur C. Clarke had predicted such a thing the age of space communication was upon us.

For many, the hero of the piece is *Telstar* and for sure there was much sadness when, a year later, it caught radiation sickness and died. But actually, my favourite link in the chain is Arthur, the huge satellite dish that was built in Cornwall to follow the satellite's progress.

He was the first open satellite dish in the world and he was a leviathan. But of course he had to be 30 metres in diameter if he was to stand a chance of pinpointing that pinprick in the sky. He also had to be fast, and he was. He may have weighed 1,180 tons but he could turn a complete circle in three minutes while moving from the horizontal through 90 degrees to the vertical.

What on earth people must have thought when he was unveiled? This huge white saucer, supported on a latticework of girders, tracking an invisible object in the sky so we in Britain could see what was going on in America . . . right now. He must have seemed like science fiction.

But he wasn't. And even more astonishingly, despite the advances in telecommunications these last 50 years, he isn't ancient history either.

Certainly, visitors to Goonhilly shouldn't mistake his lack of movement for inactivity. Nowadays he doesn't have to swivel his hips because the roving *Telstar* has been replaced by *Intelsat 903*, which does him the service of sitting still, right above the middle of the Atlantic Ocean.

Sure, Arthur has been joined over the years by a host of other dishes, all of whom are named after characters from Camelot but the king himself is still very much alive and well. In fact he is now part of the biggest machine in the world, the web of communication that spreads from below the seabed to solar-powered satellites in deep space. As a result in a normal day he can expect to handle all the banking transactions from the Caribbean, people holding for 0898 girls in California, news from New Zealand, most of the phone calls between Britain and America, and the Indian internet.

Arthur dealt smoothly with all the military radio traffic in Afghanistan and Iraq, and by firing up his motors and pointing to a new satellite he even stood in for America's wounded communications network on 11 September.

Not bad for a machine that was originally designed in the fifties to deal with one television signal or 600 phone calls. But not both at the same time.

What is bad is the state of him. I've been to all sorts of engineering sites in America. The Ames wind tunnel in California. The Stennis rocket plant in Louisiana. And, of course, Cape Canaveral in Florida. These places are just as old as Goonhilly but they're obviously well maintained and nurtured so they look like they were built yesterday.

Arthur, on the other hand, is streaked with rust and the little room behind that pointy thing in the middle of his dish looks like the storeroom at a builders' merchant.

What they're asking of him is no different from asking Jack Charlton to play for England. That Arthur can do it, and does, is testimony to the brilliance of the men who designed and built him all those years ago.

That's the thing about Big Art. He knows what the weather will be like before Burt Fish. He knows how much you spent on ice creams last time you went to St Lucia. He knows what sort of pornography they like in India. And he knows about your mistress in New Jersey. It's probably not that far from the truth to say that these days Arthur knows more about the workings of our world than God.

747

At lunchtime on 27 March 1977 a terrorist bomb exploded at Las Palmas airport in the Canary Islands. And since there were threats of more bombs in the terminal building, all incoming flights were diverted to the islands' other airport at Los Rodeos.

One of the first to land there was Captain Jacob Veldhuyzen van Zanten, aboard a KLM Jumbo. He'd been with the airline for 30 years and was responsible for training other Dutch pilots.

He was ordered by air traffic control to park his 747 on one of the taxiways and wait for Las Palmas to reopen. Suspecting that it might not take long, he initially refused to let the passengers off because then they'd have to be reloaded, and by the time he actually got them to the right place his permitted time in the cockpit would be up, and he'd be unable to fly back to Holland. He was so worried about time, in fact, that he asked for the plane to be refuelled while it was parked. This would mean he would have no need to top up the tanks at Las Palmas.

Meanwhile the airport was filling up with other planes, including a Pan Am Jumbo that was bringing a party of old people from Los Angeles to meet their cruise ship in the Canaries. This was being flown by Captain Victor Grubbs, a 57-year-old with 21,000 flying hours under his belt.

His plane was pretty special too, since it was the Clipper Victor, the first Jumbo ever to fly with passengers on board. If you watch the newsreel footage of that first flight, from New York to London on 21 January 1970, this is the plane you will see. And now, seven years later, it was bumbling around a small airport in the middle of the Atlantic looking for somewhere to park.

When Las Palmas finally reopened the Pan Am plane was boxed in by van Zanten's KLM plane and its refuelling tanker. The crew actually paced out the gap but figured that while it was close, they'd probably be better off waiting for the Dutch jet to move first.

By the time its tanks were full, at 4.26 in the afternoon, fog had settled on the airport like a big damp blanket and visibility was down to just 300 metres.

Nevertheless, the KLM jet was ordered to taxi down Runway 30 and wait at the far end for clearance to go. Meanwhile the Pan Am plane was ordered onto Runway 30, and to pull off at the third taxiway and wait until the Dutch plane had gone. At this point the fog was so bad that the air traffic controller couldn't see the planes, the Dutch couldn't see the Americans and the Americans weren't sure where they were supposed to be going.

Flight-deck recordings show confusion in the cockpit. The first officer thought he'd been asked to pull off on the first taxiway – impossible since it was a logjam of parked planes. This time the controller was clear: 'The third one, sir. One, two, three. Third one.'

By the time the confusion was cleared up the Americans, still trundling in the pea-souper towards the stationary KLM plane, had no idea how many taxiway turn-off points they'd passed. The black box recorded the captain and first officer trying to decide which was their turn-off. In the event they had missed the third taxiway and were heading for the fourth, all the while getting nearer and nearer to van Zanten.

He, in the meantime, had turned his plane around and was desperate to get going. So desperate, in fact, that he immediately opened the taps on the four engines. First Officer Klaus Meurs plainly sensed this was premature, since he was recorded saying, 'Wait. We don't have clearance.'

Van Zanten immediately applied the brakes and asked his first officer to get on the radio and get clearance. This is what the air traffic controller said: 'KL4805. You are cleared to the Papa beacon. Climb to and maintain Flight Level 90. Right turn after take-off. Proceed with heading 040 until intercepting the 325 radial from Las Palmas VOR.'

These instructions were directions for after the plane had taken off. At no point did the controller actually say they were cleared to go. But van Zanten didn't realise that and released the brakes.

As the plane began to move, towards the unseen Pan Am Jumbo, his first officer repeated the message, as is customary. 'Roger, sir, we are cleared to the Papa beacon, Flight Level 90 until intercepting the 325. We're now at take-off.'

The Jumbo has become a modern-day yardstick in the lexicon of superlatives. Like football pitches, and Nelson's Column and Wales, it is now an established unit of measurement. For instance, I was told the other day that the nets being used by modern supertrawlers are big enough to envelop a dozen 747s. I have no idea how big they are, but I sort of get the picture.

And again there was confusion. The controller took 'we're now at take-off' to mean that they were at the take-off position, not that they were actually accelerating at full tilt down the runway towards the Clipper Victor.

On board the Dutch jet were 14 crew and 234 passengers, including 48 children and 3 babies. On board the Pan Am jet there were 16 crew and 396 passengers. That's a total of 660 people. And they were on a collision course.

As the KLM jet picked up speed its flight officer, Willem Schreuder, heard the tower ask the Pan Am crew to report when they'd cleared the runway.

Assuming, incorrectly, that his captain had heard this too, he said, 'Did he not clear the runway then?'

The reply sealed everyone's fate. 'Oh yes,' said van Zanten.

On board the Pan Am plane the first officer was the first to see the KLM jet bearing down on them. 'There he is,' he shouted. 'Look at him. Goddam. That son of a bitch is coming. Get off. Get off. Get off.'

Captain Grubbs was trying. He slammed the throttles wide open but it was too late. At the last moment van Zanten had spotted the Clipper and had tried to get airborne. He made it too but not quite enough; the bottom of his plane hit the roof of the American jet. It burst into flames and smashed back into the runway. Everyone on board was killed instantly.

Aboard the Clipper the first officer reached up after the impact to shut down the howling engines, but the roof on which the switches were located had gone. So too had most of his passengers, in the initial explosion. But miraculously 70 people were pulled out alive, including all the crew of the flight deck.

The total death toll, after nine had died in hospital, was 583, making this the worst accident in the 100-year history of aviation. And therein lies the biggest problem with the 747. When one of them goes down the loss of life is always so horrific no one gives a stuff about the plane itself.

Happily, however, very few are lost. Between 1970 and 2000 1,000 Jumbos were wheeled out of Boeing's factory and only 28 have been written off in accidents.

Seven of those accidents happened on the ground while the plane was being manoeuvred, four were down to terrorists, one was destroyed by shelling in the first Gulf War and one was shot down in error by the Russians. So, of the 1,000 made only fifteen have been lost in genuine accidents. And most of those were down to human error.

To get an idea of how tough a Jumbo is, look at that photograph of the decapitated nose cone lying in a field outside Lockerbie. One of the windows is still intact.

To give you a better idea, let me take you back to the first ever 'incident' on a commercial flight. It was 1971, and for all sorts of reasons a 747 was trying to take off with too much weight from a runway at San Francisco that was too short. As it reached 165 knots it ploughed into a timber pier that ran from the end of the runway into the sea.

The steel gantries ripped through the cabin floor, destroyed the wing flaps, bent the landing gear and shattered the bulkheads. Wooden shards scythed through the tail, and through the cabin too, amputating the legs of one passenger and crushing the arm of another. But somehow the pilot managed to get the plane airborne. And even more somehow he managed to land it again. And not a single person was killed.

As a piece of design the 747 is astonishing. I mean, when the TWA Jumbo exploded shortly after leaving New York in July 1996 people assumed it must have been hit by a stray missile or a giant meteorite. The notion that a 747 had actually 'gone wrong' in some way was just too preposterous.

Actually, I still think it is preposterous. I mean, when you examine all the evidence it does look like it was blown out of the sky by someone – the US Navy was operating nearby and the Americans, let's be honest, are no strangers to the concept of friendly fire. Whatever, the US authorities say the central fuel tank exploded and, hey, these guys never lie so there you have it.

Whatever, safety is not the thing that makes the 747 stand out. The modern jet engine is now so reliable, and the on-board computers so foolproof, that all commercial airliners have a safety record that

THE 747'S WINGSPAN IS LONGER THAN THE WRIGHT BROTHERS' FIRST FLIGHT, AND ITS TAIL IS TALLER THAN A SIX-STOREY BUILDING.

makes granite look tricky and unstable. The fact is that if you flew on a plane every day, statistically it would be 13,000 years before you hit the ground in a big fireball.

Nor, actually, am I drawn to the Jumbo because of its speed, though God knows it's still the jackrabbit of the skies. The newer 777 cruises at 565 mph. The 747 is a full 20 mph faster and, over 11,000 miles, that makes a big difference to your deep-vein thrombosis.

I'm not even that excited by what the 747 did for mass transportation. It was born in the days when everyone still believed that flying was for the 'jet set' and that supersonic travel was the only way forward. No one had foreseen a time when fat women from the North would be going to Spain for £25.

No one, that is, except for the boss of Pan Am. Juan Trippe had noted the failure of America's aeroplane industry to make a supersonic jetliner and pleaded with them to go the other way, to make an enormous plane that would savage the established economies of scale.

When it finally rolled out of the Seattle factory on 30 September 1968 even the workforce was surprised at its size, and this – this – is the key to my love affair with the Jumbo. The small-boyishness of all its facts and figures. Like, for instance, did you know that on full thrust its engines hurl enough air out of the back to inflate the Goodyear airship in seven seconds?

Or how about this? It does 2.5 miles to the gallon but because it can carry over 500 people it's actually more economical, per passenger per mile, than a Ford Fiesta.

I can be even more anal if you like. It needs 1.5 miles to reach take-off speed and in a 20-year career will cover 1,500 miles going backwards. When it's being pushed back from various gates, obviously. Not when it's flying. It can't do that.

You may also be interested to know, if you're a man, that its wingspan is longer than the Wright Brothers' first flight, and that its tail is taller than a six-storey building. Also, a Jumbo could fly upside down. Though if you actually tried to turn it over in mid air, the wings would be torn off. Mind you, that said, tests have shown you can bend the wings upwards by 30 feet before they'll break.

Other things. Well, the factory where it's made is the largest building, by volume, in the world. The first Jumbo was made out of 4.5 million parts. And some experts said it should only be allowed to fly in storm-free corridors because 'there's no way something that big could weather any turbulence'.

Nearly right. So far it's transported 2.2 billion people, which is nearly 40 per cent of the world's population, and that isn't bad for a plane originally designed to carry cargo.

Although Juan Trippe had ordered planes for passengers, Boeing had agreed to the deal because they thought it could also be used as a transporter. That's why it has the hump – so the cargo could be loaded more easily via a hinged nose cone into the fuselage. See. I can go on boring for Britain about the 747 until the end of time. And so can everyone else.

The Jumbo has become a modern-day yardstick in the lexicon of superlatives. Like football pitches, and Nelson's Column and Wales, it is now an established unit of measurement. For instance, I was told the other day that the nets being used by modern supertrawlers are

I was horrified by the exchange between the pilots who hadn't heard which runway they were supposed to land on. 'Oh just follow the bloke in front,' said the captain to his young apprentice in the right-hand seat. Then we hit a flock of birds. 'Got 'em,' said the captain, but I hardly registered because I simply couldn't believe how much effort the co-pilot was having to make. He was bathed in sweat as he manhandled the big jet out of that sticky, sultry sky.

big enough to envelop a dozen 747s. I have no idea how big they are, but I sort of get the picture.

There's only one thing blokes love more than an interesting fact and that's a superlative. That's why I like the 747, because it's the biggest and the fastest and the heaviest . . . and the best.

In the beginning it had a rough ride. In the 1,013 test flights the engines had to be changed 55 times. They even overheated on the very first commercial flight, which is why the ill-fated Clipper Victor was brought in as a last-minute replacement. Then there was a recession, which coupled with the technical problems meant the 747 was originally known as the Dumbo Jet.

Oh, how things change. Most people today choose a specific flight because it suits their requirements on a particular day. Not me though. I tailor my travel arrangements so that I can go on a Jumbo.

777s are rubbish, and while I recognise that the four-engined Airbuses are astonishingly quiet they're still buses. And where's the glamour in that?

When I get on a Jumbo I'm always going somewhere exotic – they don't use them on hops to the Isle of Man – and I want a taste of that on the plane. Which is why I like the stairs. Having decided a hump for the flight deck was a good idea, there was plenty of discussion about what might be placed behind it. A hair salon was one serious suggestion. A casino was another.

It's perfect now, as the best bit of business class. Up there you don't have the sense of being a veal calf. And if the airline has its head screwed on, you're also away from the peril of a screaming baby. Up there you can convince yourself you're in an exec jet. Only you can't, of course, because a Jumbo is so much quieter.

The one place you don't want to be on a 747 is on the flight deck. We sort of assume as we slide down to the runway that all is calm and automated up there at the business end but, let me assure you, this is not so. Once I was invited to sit in the jump seat for a landing into Houston.

SO FAR IT'S TRANSPORTED 2.2 BILLION PEOPLE, WHICH IS NEARLY 40 PER CENT OF THE WORLD'S POPULATION.

Firstly, I was horrified by the exchange between the pilots who hadn't heard which runway they were supposed to land on. 'Oh just follow the bloke in front,' said the captain to his young apprentice in the right-hand seat. Then we hit a flock of birds. 'Got 'em,' said the captain, but I hardly registered because I simply couldn't believe how much effort the co-pilot was having to make. He was bathed in sweat as he manhandled the big jet out of that sticky, sultry sky.

Nowadays no passenger is allowed on a flight deck, unless you're away from America and in the free world, and I'm glad about that. I prefer to sit in blissful ignorance of how hard it is to land what is basically a big airborne bison.

And I don't want to see the pilots having a row or looking at their watches and tutting. I want to believe I'm at the mercy of a machine. Because when that machine is a 747 there's nothing to worry about. Nothing to worry about at all.

Stalingrad 1942: The appalling human cost
of defending Russia from the Nazi invasion
showed the need for a gun like the AK47.

It's the winter of 1942 and, after a thunderous trip across western Russia, the German army has arrived in the city of Stalingrad, still hopeful that they'll be in Moscow for Christmas.

However, Stalin decided this was far enough. Maybe he made this decision for tactical reasons. Stalingrad was the key to Russia's oil fields. Or maybe it was vanity. It was after all the city that bore his name. But whatever, he decided that, come what may, the Nazis would go no further.

As blizzards and biting cold descended on the ruined city, men, women and children from all over Russia were sent on trains to this hellhole and ordered to fight to the death. If you retreated, you were shot. If you failed to win a skirmish, you were shot. If you deserted, you were shot. If you were captured, you were not shot. But if you escaped and returned to you own lines, you were. Because you might have become a German spy.

Oh, and if you stood your ground and fought, you were shot. And to make matters slightly worse, half the new recruits being sent into the battlefield couldn't even shoot back because guns were in such short supply. You had to wait for a comrade who did have a gun to be shot and then nick his rifle.

As we all know, the superhuman Russian effort did eventually win the day. But the losses were simply gigantic, a point that was not lost on a young tank sergeant called Mikhail Timofeevich Kalashnikov.

At the time he was recovering in hospital from injuries sustained in another, earlier battle. And that meant he had time to reflect on the lot of his fellow soldiers. And what he decided was that in urban warfare the Germans had a massive advantage because they had machine guns. And the Soviets, largely, did not.

With a rifle you can hit a small target from many hundreds of yards away. With a machine gun you cannot. You would, in fact, have a hard job hitting a house from the front gate – the bullets go pretty much everywhere except where you're actually aiming. So, with a rifle you can kill one man. But with a machine gun you can make a whole army keep its head down.

70 MILLION HAVE BEEN SOLD. THAT MEANS THAT ONE PERSON IN 90 ACROSS THE WHOLE PLANET HAS GOT ONE.

Kalashnikov had already distinguished himself by inventing a device that counted the shells a tank had fired and now, as he recuperated from his wounds, he set about designing something that could rival the Germans' MP44. A hand-held sub-machine gun. Something that came to be known as the AK47.

It wasn't actually ready, as the name implies, until 1947, two years after Hitler's penis had been buried under the Kremlin, but that didn't stop it becoming by far and away the most successful gun in the whole of military history.

No patent was ever taken out, which meant anyone with a foundry could set up shop and make one too. And they did. AKs were produced all around the world in such vast numbers that so far 70 million have been sold. And that in turn means that one person in 90 across the whole planet has got one. And as a result of that, it is said that the AK47 has killed more people than the atomic bombs that were dropped on Hiroshima and Nagasaki.

Think of any conflict since 1947 and it's a fairly safe bet that at least one of the sides has been using AK47s. The warlords in Mogadishu, the Vietcong in Vietnam, the Republican Guard in Iraq. This half-timbered gun has been a 50-year thorn in Uncle Sam's side.

Kalashnikov set
about designing
something that could
rival the Germans'
MP44. A hand-held
sub-machine gun.
Something that
came to be known
as the AK47.

Interestingly, however, it doesn't actually do anything especially interesting. You get a 30-round magazine that fires normal 7.62mm ammunition at a rate of 600 bullets per minute. That gives you enough ammo for a three-second burst, which is about average. And there's nothing unusual about its range either. Reckon on 1,100 yards or so.

In fact it even has a few design defects, like it weighs nearly 10 lbs. That doesn't sound like much but you try carrying it around all day, in a jungle. Then there are the sights, which are too far forward on the barrel. But worse is the safety switch. To get it from 'safe' to 'single shot' you have to go through the 'fully automatic' setting. And as you move it, it gives away its Russian origins, and your position, by going 'clack'.

So there you are, trying to ease the safety off quietly for a nice, clean shot. But as you do so the target hears the mechanism and fires. You then fire back only to find you're in fully automatic mode and that you've missed.

So why then, if it's heavy, flawed and nothing special, has it been such a hit? Well, the simple answer is its simplicity. In a competition to find the least-complicated machine ever made, it would tie in first place with the mousetrap.

Pull off the back and all you'll find is the hammer and a piece of bailer twine to operate it. This is a gun, then, that's ideal for the jungle-based freedom fighter. You can bash it, crash it and bury it for months in a swamp and it will still work. The total reliability is what made the AK such a phenomenal hit. Oh, and the fact you can buy a used one from an Albanian market trader today for $3.

I dare say some of those silver-plated AKs you see slung over the shoulders of the soldiers in West Africa are a little more. But not much. I mean, the soldiers in question are usually only five years old, which means they've bought their guns, and had them customised, out of their pocket money.

Once, while I was working in Switzerland, a Hell's Angel offered me a brand-new AK47, still in its greaseproof wrapping paper, for £300. He would even have thrown in a thousand rounds of ammunition for good measure.

THE 30-ROUND MAGAZINE FIRES NORMAL 7.62MM AMMUNITION AT A RATE OF 600 BULLETS PER MINUTE. THAT GIVES YOU ENOUGH AMMO FOR A THREE-SECOND BURST.

'Here,' he said, 'try it out.' And so I did, firing at a railway sleeper maybe 60 yards away at the bottom of a quarry. The effect was astonishing. The bullets smashed the sleeper into two pieces that ended up ten feet from one another. So much, I remember thinking, for those Hollywood heroes who say 'ow' when they're hit.

Now, I know I should have been revolted by the power of this weapon. I know I should have given it back and gone on my way. But my God, what a tool. I was filled with a fervent wish to take it home and even thought about ways it might be smuggled past customs. Then I could prowl around the house at night, hoping to find a burglar.

Imagine that. Imagine squaring up to some spotty sixteen-year-old youth who's come for the video recorder, him with his potato peeler and you with an AK47. Oh the joy.

The strange thing is that no other gun would do really. I've fired the British Army's SA80 and the American M16. I've even had a go with an old Sten, and a Maxim and, best of all, a Squad Automatic Weapon, which pumped so much tracer into the Arizona desert the scrub actually caught fire.

There are people today who spend a fortune trying to look as good as Che Guevara, but he managed to look better using only a beret and a boiler suit. I bet he had a lot of sex. I also bet he had an AK47.

Each one struck me as being nothing more than a delivery device. You pull the trigger, there's a lot of noise and whatever you're aiming at isn't the same shape any more. They are like cookers – good at doing what they do but unless you're planning on shooting someone in the face, no more exciting than boiling an egg.

The AK is different. There are children in the world today named Kalash, in its honour. You will find images of it in national emblems. And closer to home, the only private number plate I've ever even half considered buying is 'AK47'. I think it would give my Volvo a bit more cred.

So what's the deal then? Why does the AK rise above all the heat and pieces? Why has it got soul when, undoubtedly, the others do not?

Well, it was born amid unimaginable strife and suffering so it has genuine working-class, hard-man origins. And unlike Cilla Black, who bangs on about her harsh Scouser upbringing from the luxury of her Thames-side mansion, the AK has never sold out. You never find an AK in the pampered hands of an American soldier, boasting about how it was brought up in a cave in Saigon. It was born to help the underdog and that's what its been doing, non-stop for nigh on 60 years.

Then we have Che Guevara, possibly the coolest man ever to have walked the planet. Yes, his real name was Ernest, but he managed to make James Dean and Steve McQueen look like a couple of nancy boys. I loathed the man's politics but I loved the T-shirt.

Even his beard worked because you knew it wasn't grown for any of the usual reasons – vanity, or laziness or insecurity. It was grown because he lived in a wood and there was no water with which to shave. There are people today who spend a fortune trying to look good, but he managed to look better using only a beret and a boiler suit. I bet he had a lot of sex. I also bet he had an AK47.

It is, after all, one of the design classics. You could frame one and hang it on the wall, and no one would want to know why you had done such a thing. Except the police perhaps.

Design is rarely art because design, when all is said and done, exists purely to make money. And yet the AK was never conceived to do that. In fact Mikhail Kalashnikov lives today on nothing more than a Soviet Army pension. And that's why his most famous creation can be called an art form. And that's what gives it soul.

Think of any conflict since 1947 and it's a fairly safe bet that at least one of the sides has been using AK47s. The warlords in Mogadishu, the Vietcong in Vietnam, the Republican Guard in Iraq. This half-timbered gun has been a 50-year thorn in Uncle Sam's side.

ZEPPELIN

In May of 1915 the Kaiser sanctioned what was possibly the most idiotic military plan in the history of warfare. He gave the go-ahead for a fleet of Zeppelin airships to mount a series of bombing raids on London and the industrial cities of Britain.

As bombers go, the Zeppelin did have one or two shortcomings. For instance, most of the hydrogen gas that filled the balloon was used to lift the craft itself off the ground. If the captain had had a big lunch, it could tip the balance and the whole thing would simply refuse to budge. This meant it could only carry a tiny number of bombs.

Also, because it was the size of a battleship and moved at no more than 40 mph just a few hundred feet from the ground, it was a fat, juicy and highly explosive target for gunners on the ground.

Happily, for the crews on board at any rate, the British placed their guns round obvious targets, factories and so on. But because Zeppelins were so hard to navigate they were always miles off course. After a few months the British government really did believe the Germans were deliberately bombing fields to destroy crops and livestock.

They weren't. They were just missing. On one raid a crew bombed the bejesus out of a Scottish castle, believing it to be a Yorkshire coal mine. On another a Zeppelin commander reported back that he'd wrecked Birmingham, when in fact he'd spent the night raining fire on Arras in northern France.

In the very first raid though, on the fishing ports Great Yarmouth and King's Lynn, there had been a modicum of success. Two people on the ground were killed, the first British civilians ever to die in an air raid. This had sent the press into a frenzy. 'The Coming of the Aerial Baby Killers,' screamed one headline. And this is exactly the reaction Germany was after.

The idea was that these huge monsters would strike such terror into the hearts of the Britischer pig dogs that we'd lose the stomach for a fight and give in immediately. But they didn't even succeed in doing that.

This was shortly after Gallipoli, the First World War was in full swing and the casualties were being measured not by the thousand but by the million. So, it's reasonable to assume that if a nation could withstand that, the systematic destruction of every able-bodied man in the land, then it'd certainly be able to handle the attention from the most inappropriate bomber of all time.

And so it turned out to be. In the first raid over London, far from cowering in underground stations, people crowded onto the rooftops for a better view of these astonishing machines. The House of Commons abandoned its business so members could rush outside for a better look. And George Bernard Shaw wrote to a friend saying, 'What is hardly credible, but true, is that the sound of the Zepp's engines was so fine, and its voyage through the stars so enchanting, that I positively caught myself hoping next night that there would be another raid.'

Frightened? Terrified? Captivated more like.

And it's not hard to see why. It wasn't the sheer size of the things, or their majesty as they made their statesmanlike progress through the forest of searchlight beams. It wasn't the drone of their Maybach engines either, or the whirr of their 17-foot mahogany propellers. No, we loved them because there's nothing we like more than the plucky chap who comes in second. The British adore a heroic failure. And the Zeppelins were more heroic and more hopeless than just about any machine ever made.

Count Ferdinand Von Zeppelin was neither an aeronaut nor an engineer. But while he was in America, during the Civil War, this German aristocrat and officer was taken up in a tethered observation balloon. And loved it. Back at home he scribbled all kinds of notes about how such a thing might be the key to flight. Steam power had been tried but it was too heavy for the gas to lift. Electric power was even worse because the batteries weighed half a ton each. It would be 25 years before a realistic form of propulsion would come along. The internal combustion engine.

Using vast chunks of his own money, the Count started work on LZ1. It was huge: 420 feet long and 38 feet in diameter, but despite the bulk it could only lift 27,000 lbs. And when you deducted the aluminium frame and the two marine engines from that you were left with a payload of just 660 lbs. Just one American, in other words.

Hitler discovered the only real use for an airship. As Goodyear and Fuji now know, everyone looks up when one of these slow-moving airborne leviathans flies over. That makes them the perfect advertising hoarding. And so it was that in the run up to the Second World War the Zeppelins were adorned with swastikas and sent around the world to drum up support for the Fatherland.

Nevertheless, in July 1900 it did actually fly. Not well enough to impress the onlookers though. The power output from the engines was less than you'd get from a VW Beetle and it bent like a banana once it was off the ground. The press said it had no value. The army people said they could see no use for it at all. And so, with all his money gone, the Count broke the ship up and sold the parts as scrap. He said afterwards his heart was broken.

However, a local king – they had such things in those days – decided to organise a state lottery to get Zeppelin going again, and so, five years later, shortly after Orville and Wilbur Wright had shown the world what a real aeroplane might look like, LZ2 took off. It crashed.

Teetering on the edge of financial collapse, Zeppelin built the LZ3, but it was too small so along came LZ4, which broke down in midair, crash-landed and then exploded. LZ5 hit a pear tree when the pilot fell asleep at the wheel. LZ6 was burned to a cinder while in its hangar and then, just after an aeroplane crossed the English Channel for the first time, along came LZ7.

LZ7 was the world's first proper passenger aircraft with luxury seating and wooden panelling in the gondola. Laden down with 23 journalists and enough caviar to feed them, it flew into a thunderstorm, reared up to 3,500 feet and then plummeted into a forest.

LZ8 never even got that far. It was wheeled out of the hangar and simply blew away. But astonishingly, and largely thanks to an enthusiastic public, the money kept dribbling in and the Count kept going.

Due, again, to public opinion, even the sceptical German Navy invested in a couple. The first crashed into the sea, killing the 15 souls on board, and the second blew up on a test flight, killing 28. Then came the war, in which further Zeppelins went about their business of bombing fields and generally cheering up the British.

The last of the wartime bombers was enormous. Seven hundred feet long with a capacity of nearly 2.2 million cubic feet of hydrogen, it could carry 3.5 tons of bombs and fly higher and faster than any airship before. It really was a technological marvel. But there was

LZ1 COULD ONLY LIFT 27,000 LBS, AND WHEN YOU DEDUCTED THE ALUMINIUM FRAME AND THE TWO MARINE ENGINES FROM THAT YOU WERE LEFT WITH A PAYLOAD OF JUST 660 LBS. JUST ONE AMERICAN, IN OTHER WORDS.

a drawback. Because it was so large it was even easier to hit, and it was, diving in a fireball into the sea.

After the war, with the factory in ruins, Count Zeppelin dead from old age and aeroplane technology coming on in leaps and bounds, they kept on making them, a small but enthusiastic team believing that maybe, just maybe, they did have a role in long-haul flight. It was even suggested the Empire State Building could be used as a mooring tower. But after the *Hindenburg* mysteriously exploded when coming in to land in America passengers were understandably wary.

Hitler described them perfectly. 'The whole thing always seems to me like an inventor who claims to have discovered a cheap new kind of floor covering which looks marvellous, shines forever, and never wears out. But he adds that there is one disadvantage. It must not be walked on with nailed shoes and nothing hard must ever be dropped on it because, unfortunately, it's made of high explosive.'

It was Hitler, however, who discovered the only real use for an airship. As Goodyear and Fuji now know, everyone looks up when one of these slow-moving airborne leviathans flies over. That makes them the perfect advertising hoarding. And so it was that in the run up to the

The *Graf Zeppelin* was the mother of all airships, 787 feet long and 115 feet high. Imagine Canary Wharf, on its side, floating over your head.

Second World War the Zeppelins were adorned with swastikas and sent around the world to drum up support for the Fatherland.

But in the middle of all this heroic failure there was one airship that did manage to achieve something truly remarkable. A voyage every bit as magical and as hazardous as Scott's or Cook's. A journey, for paying passengers, right round the world.

The year was 1929, the cost of a ticket, in today's money, would have been £50,000, and the ship in question was LZ127, the *Graf Zeppelin*.

This was the mother of all airships, 787 feet long and 115 feet high. Imagine Canary Wharf, on its side, floating over your head . . . And yet, from inside the gondola the 60 people on board would have had no sense of this gigantism. The salon was small and narrow; the cabins were smaller still, and had to be shared. But this was the twenties, so it was far from spartan.

Everyone dressed for dinner, and can you imagine that? Dining on fine wines and exotic cheeses while floating in almost complete silence over vast parts of the world that had never been seen from the air before. Russia, for instance. And then, after dinner, as the moonlit tundra drifted by outside the picture windows, dancing the Charleston to the sound of a gramophone that, despite the weight limitations, had been smuggled on board.

People had been on magnificent journeys before this. But while the destination or the route had always been new and exciting the craft that took them there, be it a ship or a sledge, was always tried and tested. The round-the-world adventure in the *Graf* was the other way around. The passengers were not going anywhere exciting; they would after all end up where they'd started. It was the craft they were using that made the difference. It was the craft that mattered.

Every day the journalists on board would send their copy home by carrier pigeon. And it really was purple prose. One, Lady Grace Hay-Drummond-Hay, the only girl on board, came up with this little nugget: 'The *Graf Zeppelin* is more than just machinery, canvas and aluminium. It has a soul.'

After the journey was completed, in just twelve days, the captain in particular, Hugo Eckener, was feted as a hero. But for me, the real star of the show was the machine itself.

I've flown round the world three times in Boeings and Airbuses, and on each occasion I discovered the meaning of true misery. Those long, endless, droning hours over mile after mile after mile of ocean, with nothing to do except watch the blood clots in your legs shake themselves loose, are enough to drive a man insane. But if I were asked tomorrow to go round again on an airship, I'd be there like a cartoon cat.

There's something baleful about an airship, something rather sad and gloomy. Like Eeyore in the 'Pooh' stories, who can't help being a donkey, they can't help being full of explosive gas and ridiculously susceptible to the vagaries of the weather. They were hamstrung by the foolishness of man and had to make do.

I see them as environmentalists might see a whale. Far too large and cumbersome, roaming the vast ocean of air, at the mercy of whatever currents might come their way. And communicating with pigeons in the same idiotic way that a whale communicates by humming. And yet, when you see a whale, and I did once, off Hawaii, you can't help but stop and gawp.

They certainly gawped when the *Graf* flew by on its epic voyage. Half a million turned out to watch it in Tokyo, for instance. And they kept on staring in silent wonderment in the subsequent years as it toured the world, a vast silvery grey advertisement for the Nazis.

It was, however, the Nazis who killed it off. Goering, displaying the humanitarian streak for which he was so infamous, ordered that the *Graf* be broken up for scrap. A sad end, and that's the point. Had it just been another machine no one would give a damn. But we do, for exactly the reason Lady Hay-Drummond-Hay identified back in 1929. The *Graf* was more than a machine. The *Graf* had a soul.

FLYING
SCOTSMAN

Trainspotters. You still see them today, occasionally. Hunched over their Tupperware sandwich boxes and their soup at the end of railway platforms, their anorak hoods pulled tight to keep out the worst of the rain and the wind. And one word comes into your mind: why?

If I'm drunk, I can just about understand the mentality of the planespotter. There are all sorts of military aircraft to jot down in your notebook. But there are no fighter trains, no stealth locomotives. These days a train is a train is a train. A good train is one that arrives on time; a bad train is one that doesn't turn up at all.

In the olden days, when there were lots of different railway companies and no such thing as economies of scale, it was a world of Jenny Agutter appearing out of the steam and Bernard Cribbins watering the station geraniums. Back then there were express trains, and locomotives used to haul coal, and the ones you saw in Yorkshire were completely different from the ones you saw in South Wales. You could meet your weird-beard mates in the snug bar of The Broken Conrod and reminisce about the day you saw the Atlantic Class 4-6-2 in the WRONG livery!!! There was a point to trainspotting. Not a very big one, I admit, and not a very sharp one either, but a point nevertheless.

Now though, the spottiest teenagers can spend their evenings downloading pornography from the internet. In fact if push came to shove, I bet you could only name one of the 660,000 steam locomotives that have been made around the world.

The Gresley Pacific 4472. Better known as the *Flying Scotsman*.

For those who were born in Doncaster – Kevin Keegan, Diana Rigg and, er, me – it's a bit galling to know that the town's most famous son is, in fact, a train, and not a very good one either.

It was chosen to represent the London & North Eastern Railway company at the 1924 British Empire Exhibition, not because it was their finest achievement but because they needed *something* and the *Scotsman* was broken at the time.

After the show it was repaired and selected to represent the LNER again, in a speed-and-economy race against the best of the best from the Great Western Railway. The northern boy turned out to be slower and more coal hungry than its southern rival.

Of course, the *Flying Scotsman*'s designers and owners said this was irrelevant. As was the way with the world's steamship companies, they said they didn't go in for speed records because this would mean pushing the machinery beyond its limit and that would be dangerous. Yeah right.

In fact they quietly took their engine back to its Doncaster birthplace and fettled it a bit to make it faster. And what's more, they fitted a corridor in the coal tender that was dragged behind the engine so the crew could leave the footplate of the locomotive and reach the front carriage without having to stop. This meant driver changes could be done on the move.

And this meant that in 1928 the *Flying Scotsman* set a record by doing 392.7 miles from King's Cross to Edinburgh. Non-stop. In a whisker over eight hours. The press went mad. The public fainted. The *Flying Scotsman* had started to make a name for itself.

It was even chosen as the star of Britain's first ever talking movie, called *The Flying Scotsman*. I *could* tell you what it was about. But that would be like trying to explain *The Matrix*, so I won't bother. Suffice it to say that as the thirties dawned the *Flying Scotsman* was a national icon.

But then disaster. News filtered through from Germany of a new diesel locomotive that had just covered the 178 miles from Berlin to Hamburg at an incredible average speed of 77.4 mph. It was one thing being beaten by a bunch of southern poufs, but quite another being beaten by the Hun.

So, to show Jerry who was boss, the *Flying Scotsman* set off for Leeds. It averaged just 72 mph on the way north and failed again on the way south. But while attempting one record it inadvertently broke another. It became the first train, ever, to do 100 mph. 147 tons doing the ton. This time it was a lead item on the BBC's nine o'clock news and people listening died of excitement.

After the glory days 4472 became just another train plodding up and down the East Coast line until, by 1961, he was just another

The *Flying Scotsman* set
a record by doing 392.7 miles
from King's Cross to Edinburgh.
Non-stop. In a whisker over
eight hours. The press went
mad. The public fainted. The
Flying Scotsman had started
to make a name for itself.

The *Flying Scotsman* certainly had something. Maybe it's because he huffed and puffed, giving the sense that a) he was a dragon and that b) he was alive. More likely, though, I was drawn to his beauty. Francis Bacon once said there is no beauty that hath not some strangeness to its proportion. Cameron Diaz proves that – she's got a mouth like a slice of watermelon. But the *Flying Scotsman* proves it to be wrong. There is no strangeness at all. He is exquisite to behold, partly because he is so nicely balanced and partly because he seems to shout, 'I AM VERY POWERFUL.'

THE *FLYING SCOTSMAN* WAS THE FIRST TRAIN, EVER, TO DO 100 MPH. 147 TONS DOING THE TON.

engine. He was even overlooked by a commission set up to decide which locomotives should be preserved in museums as diesel took over. They said there was only room for one Gresley Pacific and that would be the *Mallard*, which held the speed record by that time.

And so, on 14 January 1963, with a whopping 2.1 million miles on the clock, the *Flying Scotsman* was withdrawn from service. No one cared. Except for the men on railway platforms, who downed their Tupperware and demanded action. 'You can't just scrap him,' they wailed.

Happily, their protest reached the attention of a Doncaster boy called Alan Pegler, who bought the engine for £3,000 – only slightly less than half what it had cost to build.

He carried on running him, as a sort of joyride experience, and I'm glad about that because it meant I got a chance to see him thundering around from time to time. Somewhere, although I've no idea where, I have a collection of pennies that I put on the line to be squashed by the *Flying Scotsman*.

It's funny. I was only seven at the time – what were my parents doing allowing me to play on railway lines? – but I knew the *Flying Scotsman* was special somehow. I didn't know about the speed and endurance records. I didn't know about the British Empire Exhibition. And to be honest I preferred the Buck Rogers Deltic diesel engines that were belting through Doncaster in those days.

And yet, the *Flying Scotsman* certainly had something. Maybe it's because he huffed and puffed, giving the sense that a) he was a dragon and that b) he was alive. More likely, though, I was drawn to his beauty.

Francis Bacon once said there is no beauty that hath not some strangeness to its proportion. Cameron Diaz proves that – she's got a mouth like a slice of watermelon. But the *Flying Scotsman* proves it to be wrong. There is no strangeness at all. He is exquisite to behold, partly because he is so nicely balanced and partly because he seems to shout, 'I AM VERY POWERFUL.'

Over the years the *Flying Scotsman* has travelled the world and been owned by pretty well everyone except my wife, and possibly Kate Moss. As I write he's for sale again, for a not inconsiderable £2.5 million.

That may seem a lot for something that no longer has a purpose, even if he is a piece of Britain's engineering heritage. But he is not simply a machine. Like an Aston Martin DB7 or an F-16 fighter, he works as an art form too, a piece of sculpture. So what if you can't go anywhere in him any more. Put him in your garden and spend your days just looking at him.

B-52

In the autumn of 1962 President Kennedy was locked in a bunker discussing the new Russian missiles on Cuba and what might be done about them, President Khrushchev was in Moscow wondering if America's naval blockade had any teeth, and the world was poised for nuclear war.

It was a simple problem. The Americans didn't want Russian missiles 90 miles off the coast of Florida. But the Russians couldn't see what the problem was since there were American missiles in Turkey, just 150 miles from its own borders.

Winning this argument meant having a war. So what was needed was a solution where no one lost. And that seemed to be just about impossible.

Since I was two at the time, my biggest concern was . . . actually, I can't remember what my biggest concern was, but it probably had something to do with biscuits. My mum and dad, however, have subsequently admitted that they were crapping themselves.

I don't think this shows them to be woolly-headed liberals. They were simply the parents of two small children and felt that both of us were about to be incinerated. This gave them a sense that the misery and pain of childbirth had been for nothing, because everything was about to end.

Today all we have to worry about are a few disgruntled Algerian youths who maybe have a bit of poison. Back then the world was threatened by two superpowers, each of which had enough nuclear bombs to destroy the world ten times over. It must have been terrifying.

And the symbol of all this hate and envy between Russia and America has to be the B-52 bomber, a plane conceived and built with only one purpose in mind. To drop atom bombs on men, women and children. So by rights we should look at it today with the same venom and hatred that we look at the swastika.

And yet.

A few years ago, long after the Berlin Wall had come down and America and Russia had made public man love, I was at the Davis-Monthan Air Force Base just outside Tucson in Arizona. This remarkable place is known as the boneyard because it's here that the US Air Force stores its unwanted planes.

The climate is just right – warm and dry – and the soil is heavily alkaline so the aluminium remains untouched by the passage of time. Even the hundred or so F-4 Phantoms that were stored there looked brand spanking new.

But it was not the condition of the planes that startled me most of all. It was the sheer numbers. Hundreds and hundreds of every conceivable aircraft from bombers to helicopters were lined up, some waiting to be scrapped, some waiting to be sold and some waiting for a war. These had had their sensitive equipment removed, along with all their oils and fluids, and were just sitting there, in the dry desert air, looking rather forlorn.

But it was at the back of the base, probably five miles from the front entrance, that I found the most amazing sight of them all. A huge guillotine was on its long murderous descent straight into the left wing stem of a B-52 bomber. The massive plane staggered, the wing fell off and then it seemed to stand upright again, waiting for the next blow. This time its other wing was severed, and then the fuselage was simply cut in half.

This was another example of the Strategic Arms Reduction Treaty (START) at work. It was another piece of the nuclear jigsaw being removed and, thanks to the endlessly clear skies down there in Arizona, the Russian spy satellites would have had a good view of the action. Doubtless they were pleased over in Moscow as they looked at their monitors. I should have been pleased too. But somehow I wasn't. I was sad, because despite everything I like the B-52. Or as it's known in the American Air Force, the BUFF. The Big Ugly Fat Fucker.

It's hard to explain why but I think it has something to do with the innocence of machinery. The bomber never knew that it had been designed to drop atom bombs or what those bombs could do. It didn't ask to wreak such havoc in Vietnam, or the Gulf or Kosovo. It was simply asked to take off with its belly full of what, so far as it was concerned, may as well have been heavy eggs and fly for anything up

Hundreds and hundreds of every conceivable aircraft from bombers to helicopters were lined up, some waiting to be scrapped, some waiting to be sold and some waiting for a war. These had had their sensitive equipment removed, along with all their oils and fluids, and were just sitting there, in the dry desert air, looking rather forlorn.

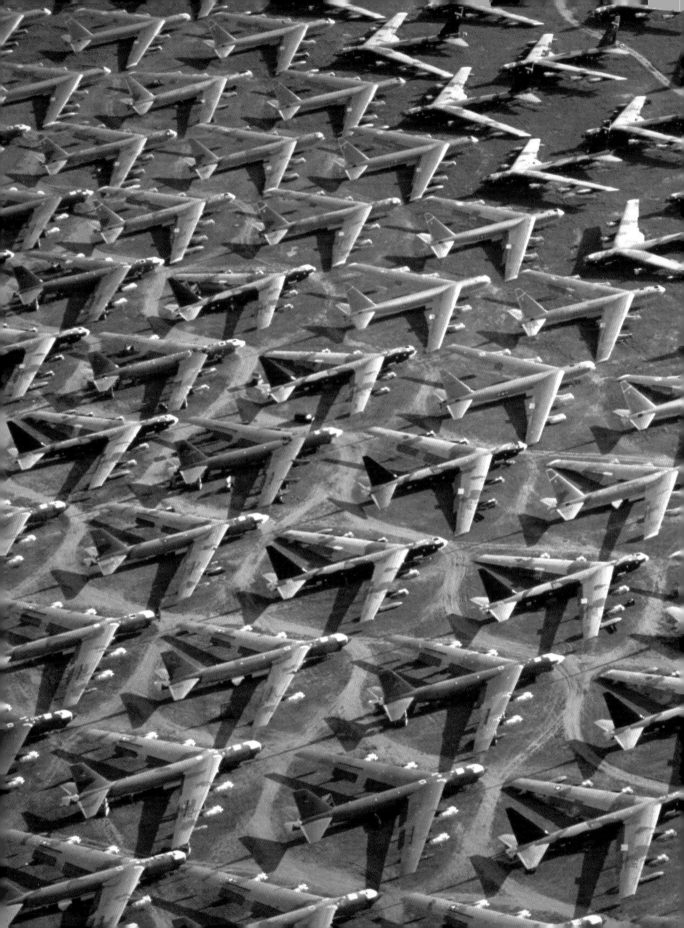

to 45 hours – non-stop. It had performed this task, well, for 40 years and now, for no reason it could fathom, they were cutting its arms off.

The story of the B-52 is an epic, with its genesis in those busy, confusing days after the Second World War. In the blink of an eye we'd gone from a piston-engined world with conventional bombs to nuclear power and jets. So no one seemed to know for sure what sort of planes might be needed, especially as the new threat seemed to be coming from Russia of all places.

Boeing had several attempts to make a long-range bomber for the post-war era but each time they were told to go away and make it faster. 'And while you're at it, can you make it carry more?' So they substituted the turboprop engines for six Pratt and Whitney jets, swept the wings back by 20 degrees, and then they were ready.

'Yes,' said the military. 'But can you make it faster?' So they swept the wings back by 35 degrees and added two more jets, bringing the total to eight. There was so much on the wings at this point in fact that each was fitted with a small wheel on the tip to stop it dragging on the ground.

By this time Convair was in the race, offering the top brass the biggest plane the world had ever seen, or would see until the C-5 Galaxy came along a full sixteen years later. Theirs was not only bigger than Boeing's but stronger, capable of carrying a heavier load and, best of all, much, much cheaper. But the military decided to go with the B-52 for one simple reason. With all those engines, it was 100 mph faster, and speed, they sort of knew, was going to be everything.

And so in 1952, with the wings swept back even more, the BUFF emerged from its hangar in the dead of night under a sheet. Already Cold War paranoia was beginning to settle on the land like a big itchy blanket.

It was huge. The tail fin stood as tall as a five-storey building, and the wing span beggared belief. At 185 feet, it's only ten feet shorter than the width of a modern-day Boeing 747.

After the inaugural flight Boeing test pilot Tex Johnson told waiting dignitaries that it was 'a hell of a good aeroplane'. But he was lying. Later that day he told Boeing engineers that pilots of the B-52 would

THE LAST B-52 WAS MADE IN THE MID SIXTIES. THEY WILL REMAIN IN SERVICE UNTIL 2045. SO, BY THE TIME THE LAST B-52 FLIES IT WILL VERY NEARLY BE AN ANTIQUE.

need new flying suits because 'if we are going to have to manhandle this son of a bitch around, we're going to have arms bigger than our legs'.

Quickly modifications were made, but already it was beginning to look like a botch job, a machine that had started out as one thing and then been converted into something that was no good, and then repaired to make it bearable. No one back then in 1952 could possibly have known that the BUFF would still be operational 50 years later.

Even though the last of the 744 B-52s was made in the mid sixties, when I was still worrying about biscuits, they will remain in service until 2045. So, by the time the last B-52 flies it will very nearly be an antique. And that, surely, makes it one of the most impressive machines ever made.

What makes it doubly impressive is that it's never really done the job for which it was designed. It's never dropped an A- or an H-bomb in anger. But there was a time, of course, when everyone though it would have to . . .

In 1960 the Americans figured they would have fifteen minutes to respond to a nuclear attack, so the Air Force was ordered to make sure its B-52s could be armed and airborne within a quarter of an hour of

The B-52 was huge. The tail fin stood as tall as a five-storey building, and the wing span beggared belief. At 185 feet, it's only ten feet shorter than a modern-day Boeing 747.

the balloon going up. This was a tall order. It meant crews had
to sleep next to their planes, and the A-bombs had to be kept in
the fuselage rather than in safe bunkers. That was a security
nightmare, but worse was to come.

Just three years later the Americans realised they wouldn't
have fifteen minutes at all. This was the era of the intercontinental
ballistic missile, which meant they'd actually have four minutes'
warning. So they ordered the Air Force to make sure the B-52s
could be up there and fighting back just 240 seconds after the
hotline phone rang.

Astonishingly, the Air Force tried to comply. Pyrotechnic cartridge
starters were fitted so that all eight engines could be ignited at once.
Water injection was added to give more power. But the planes were
now taking off in plumes of black smoke, and four minutes still
remained an impossible target.

There was nothing for it. There had to be at least a dozen B-52s
up there, at 40,000 feet, with nuclear bombs on board, 7 days a week,
24 hours a day. That meant refuelling them in flight and that was
a nightmare. They were going to fly in close formation with a tanker,
when their bellies were full of nuclear arms.

How they managed to do this for ten years without a single accident
is baffling. Or rather it would be if it were true.

In fact a B-52 did hit its refuelling tanker over Kentucky in 1959, and
it did crash with two nukes on board. Happily there was no radiation leak.

But on 17 January 1966 it happened again. A B-52 hit its tanker,
this time over Spain, and this time with four bombs on board. Two
did spring leaks when they hit the ground prompting the biggest
spring clean Spain had ever seen.

Guess what. In January 1968, over the Greenland ice pack,
a nuclear-armed B-52 crashed while trying to perform an emergency
landing and, again, there was fall-out. But this time the US decided
enough was enough. By this stage they'd worked out how to put
nuclear bombs on submarines so there was really no need to
have them in the air any more.

DURING THE COLD WAR THERE HAD TO BE AT LEAST A DOZEN B-52S UP THERE, AT 40,000 FEET, WITH NUCLEAR BOMBS ON BOARD, 7 DAYS A WEEK, 24 HOURS A DAY.

It looked like the end of the road for the B-52. Maybe a few could be used, as they always had been, as airborne launch pads for NASA and Air Force experiments, but its role as a dealer of death seemed to be over.

Not for long. Someone had already realised that, with a few changes to its belly, it could be converted into a conventional bomber. Which would help swing the balance of power America's way in the Vietnam conflict. 'Yes,' everyone thought, 'a plane this big could carry 60,000 lbs of conventional bombs and that'll show the slopes a thing or two.'

To begin with things went badly. On the very first mission in South-East Asia they lost their refuelling tanker, and then two planes hit each other killing eight of the twelve men on board. The rest did make it to the target, where they unleashed hundreds of bombs. But by the time this happened the enemy had gone home, so the mission, which had cost $20 million, resulted in eight dead Americans, two dead North Vietnamese, two downed bombers and a broken rice store.

But this wasn't the plane's fault. This was simply the usual American problem of overconfidence.

Eventually, though, they worked it out and the B-52's raids became so accurate they could happily drop bombs within 300 yards of friendly troops on the ground. An art they seem to have lost.

'Yes,' said the military. 'But can you make it faster?' So Boeing swept the wings back by 35 degrees and added two more jets, bringing the total to eight.

IN VIETNAM B-52 RAIDS BECAME SO ACCURATE THEY COULD HAPPILY DROP BOMBS WITHIN 300 YARDS OF FRIENDLY TROOPS ON THE GROUND.

We've all seen those films of bombs tumbling out of B-52s over Vietnam and I guess we've all speculated on what it must have been like to be underneath such an onslaught. Well, to begin with, not too bad it seems. On 11 April 1966 (my sixth birthday) 30 B-52s with 24 1,000-lb bombs in their bellies and 24 750-lb bombs under their wings bombed the bejesus out of a Vietnamese supply route. It was closed for just twenty hours.

Two weeks later the bombers were back, leaving 32 craters in the road. All of which were filled in within a day. The Americans, for a while, stopped bombing the North Vietnamese.

At first the top brass hadn't wanted to put a B-52 in serious harm's way because losing one would have been a propaganda boost for the enemy. But by 1972 they were in danger of losing the war, so what was the odd plane.

The B-52s were ordered to bomb the far north of the country, overflying missile sites all the way. Providing, that is, they could get off the ground the first place. They would actually dip as they flew off the end of the clifftop runway in Guam, and then fight for altitude, or at least to 700 feet, where the downward-pointing ejector seats would have a chance of working.

The operation, known as Linebacker, was so ferocious that the North Vietnamese negotiating team at the peace talks in Paris started to adopt a more positive tone. As a result the raids were stopped, which gave the NVA a chance to repair their anti-aircraft sites, which in turn brought belligerence back to the peace talks.

When the Vietnamese walked away from the table in December 1972 Nixon told his aides, 'Those bastards have never been bombed like they're going to be bombed this time.' In other words, he was using the B-52 as an instrument of diplomacy.

In the course of the Vietnam War no one can say how much good the bombers did because America lost. Had they not been there, would it have made any difference? Who knows? What we can say is two were scrapped after sustaining battle damage and seventeen were shot down.

Today one of these – or what's left of it – sits outside the Vietnamese War Museum in Hanoi. I'd love to tell you I was moved by the twisted and smashed wreckage but I'd just been inside the museum itself, where I'd seen the damage done by those B-52 raids. I'd seen pickled babies with two heads and suffering like you simply wouldn't believe, and you know what . . . the mangled plane seemed to me to have got what it deserved.

It is to Vietnam's eternal credit that this place is now called the 'War Museum'. When I was there it was called the 'War Crimes Museum'. They've forgiven the Americans and I, as we've seen, have forgiven the plane.

That said, as they took off from the base in Gloucestershire and flew right over my house on their way to Iraq recently I must admit they sent a shiver down my spine. It was strange knowing that in s even hours' time, when I was coming inside to escape the night's chill, those planes would be dropping 60,000 lbs of explosive diplomacy on Baghdad.

That's the strangest thing of all about the long-range bomber. With its cruise missiles and its laser-guided bombs, it's designed to bring utter devastation to a city. And yet, because of its range, it lives in a birdsong world far removed from this shock and awe. That makes such a thing a little bit alien, a little bit frightening.

For fifty years the B-52 has reminded everyone that behind our ordinary lives the world is not a safe place. And by announcing that it'll be flying until the middle of this century the powers that be are telling us they don't expect things to improve any time soon.

The B-52 was conceived and built with only one purpose in mind. To drop atom bombs on men, women and children. So by rights we should look at it today with the same venom and hatred that we look at the swastika.

HOOVER DAM

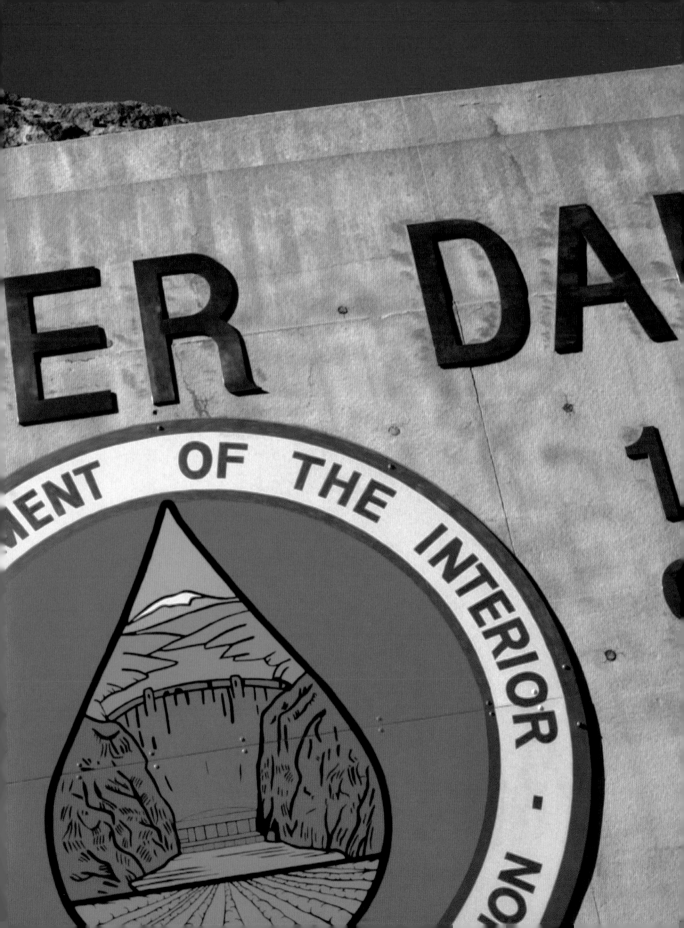

The Hoover Dam was the first structure to contain more masonry than the Great Pyramid at Giza. But it's rather more than 6.6 million tons of concrete. It's rather more than a white wall, somewhere in the middle of nowhere. Yes, it's spectacular; yes, it is a demonstration of man's power and ingenuity. But what it is most of all is an engine – a big one.

Its seventeen motors, each of which weighs more than 100 tons and turn at 90 revs per minute, generate around 3 million horsepower, which is enough oomph to provide 1.8 million people in the western United States with electricity. And yet the strangest, and best, thing about this colossus is that it runs on water. It is powered by the Colorado River.

The Colorado has brought down so much silt and soil from the mountains over the years that it has quite literally changed the shape of America. This silt has been deposited in the sea in such vast quantities that it's become land. Today, the Colorado River's journey is 150 miles longer because the Gulf of California is now that much further away. But altering the shape of a continent was just a starter for this truly amazing waterway.

You see, it's not just a silt-delivery system. It is also a moody and temperamental bastard with a punch that mere mortals find hard to comprehend . . . Once I had some luck at the black-jack tables in Las Vegas and decided to spend the winnings on a short helicopter flight to the river's greatest achievement – the Grand Canyon.

As we left the city limits the pilot flew lower and lower until the skids were just a few feet from the desert floor and then bang. In an instant we were a mile high. My stomach turned, my eyes became saucers, I think my teeth may have moved about a bit. I had seen the Canyon in films and pictures but nothing – nothing – can prepare you for the shock of seeing it, live, for the first time. Its vastness quite simply beggars belief.

Far, far below there appeared to be grassy banks to the river, a blaze of green in this barren and hostile land. But as the Jet Ranger went down it became apparent that they were in fact trees. That's what the Grand Canyon does to your sense of perspective. It turns a mighty Scots pine, or whatever they were, into a blade of grass.

EACH MOTOR WEIGHS MORE THAN 100 TONS AND TURNS AT 90 REVS PER MINUTE. TOGETHER THEY GENERATE AROUND 3 MILLION HORSEPOWER.

After we landed I strolled over to the river that had made this giant axe-smash in the crust of the earth and I wondered. How? It had no access to nuclear weapons, not that there's a nuke in anyone's arsenal that could have created such a chasm. So how did it do such a thing?

It didn't look like much, a sort of benign brown worm really, a silted-up slither. They used to say in the olden days that, thanks to the silt, it was too thick to drink and too thin to plough. But then, this was June. This was the quiet time.

In the spring things are rather different. In the spring all of the snow that has fallen on the western side of the Rockies – and there's a lot – starts to melt. From an area of 1,000 square miles a million streams are created, which trickle with increasing force into the Colorado. Now it's carrying billions and billions of gallons of water a day. Now it's a raging, seething torrent. Now it can cut through volcanic rock as though it's not there at all.

For centuries man had simply not bothered with the Colorado at all. When it was quiet it was useless. When it was noisy it had the power to smash entire mountains.

There's something strangely odd about a straight, man-made edge in this barren and craggy terrain. It's as out of place as a footprint on the moon or the rusting hulk of the *Titanic* on the seabed. It shouldn't belong, and yet, somehow, it does.

But since the beginning of the nineteenth century man had begun
to develop an ego. In Britain the likes of Stephenson and Brunel and
Telford really were going boldly where no one had gone before. Giant
steamships made from iron were conquering the seas. Trains were
bringing cities closer together, bridges were linking communities
that had been split since the dawn of time.

There was a sense we were unstoppable and that nothing couldn't
be tamed. And so the Americans decided to have a go at mastering the
Colorado. A young surveyor and engineer called Charles Rockwood –
Brunel he wasn't – realised that the Colorado desert was at a lower
elevation than the Colorado River. So he reckoned that if he built
a tributary, gravity would carry water to the desert, making it rich
and fertile.

Brilliant! Uninhabitable desert would be transformed into pasture.
Land prices would rocket. Rockwood would make a fortune.

He found himself a wealthy backer in Los Angles, changed the
name of the Colorado Desert, which sounded a bit bleak, to Imperial
Valley, which sounded much better, and people began to buy plots.
The first water began to flow along his canal on 14 May 1901, and for
a while things looked good. By this stage 7,000 people had moved
in and the agricultural production went far beyond even the most
optimistic predictions.

But old Charlie Boy hadn't thought things through. You see, it wasn't
only water that was flowing into his canal. There was so much silt that
just three years after the project began a four-mile section of the canal
was completely bunged up. As a result everyone's crops died that year.

But a few dead fields of wheat were nothing compared to what
happened next.

Rockwood figured the solution – God knows why – was to build a
second canal. He didn't know it but he was about to unleash the beast.
He was walking into a nightmare of epic proportions.

Almost immediately after the second canal opened in the March of
1905 the spring melt waters appeared and a small lake began to form
in a place called Salton. They called it the Salton Sink and figured there

was time to think what should be done. But there wasn't. Just six months later the Salton Sink covered 150 square miles and was 60 feet deep. And water was still flooding in at the rate of 150,000 cubic feet – a second.

At this rate they would have an inland ocean on their hands.

To make matters worse, engineers had noticed that a small waterfall at the lake's exit point was growing – and growing fast. The ground onto which the water was falling was being washed away, so that within weeks the waterfall was 100 feet high. And the cascade flowing over it was cutting a channel at random through the desert at the rate of one mile a day.

They probably thought this was no big deal. They probably thought that, eventually, they'd find a way to cut off supply to the second canal. But actually the clock was ticking – geologists who visited the site worked out that pretty soon the waterfall would be one mile high and that the course of the Colorado would be changed for ever, with catastrophic consequences.

The government stepped in and spent $3 million and two years rectifying Rockwood's hopelessness.

Now you'd have expected after this debacle that Washington would have been wary of any projects with the Colorado, but just 22 years later, in 1929, President Hoover approved a plan to build a dam. A dam that today bears his name.

The timing simply couldn't have been better, because just six months after the approval was given the stock market crashed and the Great Depression swept across the land. Unemployment rocketed to 25 per cent and as a result there was no trouble at all finding men willing to work on what was almost certainly the most barbaric engineering feat of the twentieth century.

The site chosen for the dam was in Boulder Canyon, which was a barren piece of nowhere. Las Vegas, built by workers on the transcontinental railway line, was a two-bit whorehouse with a few bars, and anyway it was twenty miles away.

As work began and men began to flood in with their families, a tented village sprang up on the banks of the river. They called it

Its seventeen motors generate enough oomph to provide 1.8 million people in the western United States with electricity. And yet the strangest, and best, thing about this colossus is that it runs on water. It is powered by the Colorado River.

Ragtown and it was horrific. No public order, no sanitation, no respite from the fierce summer heat and no running water. Still, life in the camp was five-star luxury compared to life on the dam site.

First of all, the river had to be temporarily diverted so the dam could be built. That meant four giant tunnels, each 56 feet in diameter and three-quarters of a mile long, had to be blasted through the 700-foot-high walls of the canyon. The air inside these tunnels was a mix of dust from the explosions and fumes from the trucks that took the waste away.

As the men began to collapse and die, many tried to pressurise the company building the dam to use electric vehicles instead, but the company knew they had everyone over a barrel. Complain and you lost your job. And you weren't going to get another.

Only when the workforce was told their $5-a-day wages were to be cut was there a strike. But it was over in days.

As the tunnels were being built, other men were sent over the edge of the canyon to prepare the cliff faces for the dam. These guys were known as 'high scalers' and they spent their days dangling on ropes, blasting stubborn bits of rock with dynamite and chiselling the easier parts.

Some died when rocks from above fell on their heads. Some died when they fell onto the rocks below. But despite this, everyone kept working and going home to Ragtown at night. Because there was no option.

Time was of the essence. The company had to get the river flowing through the tunnels by the winter of 1932, when the water was low. Or they'd be stuck for a whole year. And if they hadn't completed the bypass system by October 1933, they'd be facing penalties of $3,000 a day.

The pace of work was therefore furious. Site boss Frank Crowe drove his men so hard that if a man died, he was simply left. 'He can't do any harm now,' the foremen would say, as the endless stream of machinery and men trundled by. Trucks carrying rocks blasted from the tunnels were made to reverse down narrow canyon roads so they didn't have to waste time turning round at the top. Drivers developed the art of backing up with the door open, so they could jump if the truck toppled over the side. It was worse than hell out there.

And the summer of 1931 was the hottest on record. Even at the camp women and children were dying of heat exhaustion. At the site it was 130 degrees, and it was not unusual for the workers' body temperatures to rise to 110 degrees.

And then the river decided to show everyone who was boss. It had been meandering past the site for months, but almost as though it sensed what was being done it girded its loins and went berserk.

After the water had receded the entire site was covered in a thick layer of silt and mud. So Crowe made everyone work even harder and even faster to get back on schedule. And he made it. On time, a 750-foot-wide temporary dam was made, forcing the river into his new tunnels and, for the first time in millions of years, the floor of the Boulder Canyon was dry. Work on the main dam could begin.

Now you might think that this would be simple. You'd just need a lot of concrete. But unfortunately, when concrete sets there's a chemical reaction within it that generates heat. So if it were to be poured into the canyon in one continuous stream, engineers figured, the dam would take 120 years to cool down.

It was therefore made in blocks 60 feet by 5, all interlaced, until on 1 February 1935 there it was; 726 feet high, 660 feet thick at the base and more than 1,200 feet across, easily the largest dam in the world. And it had been built in one of the most inhospitable places on earth, in five years, for less than $50 million. The electricity made there today generates that much cash every three months.

The temporary dam was removed, and the Colorado once again tried to resume its normal course. But the wall held it back, and back, and back. It rose, drowning Ragtown, the tented village, to become a reservoir that sits now like a massive blue splodge on the borders of Nevada and Arizona. It's called Lake Mead and it contains enough water to drown the state of Pennsylvania to a depth of a foot. There are 9.2 trillion gallons sitting there, waiting to be sucked through the dam's intake pipes, past the turbines and turned into power we can actually use.

The best thing about
the Hoover Dam is the way
it looks. With its art deco
intake towers and that
preposterous slope, which
seems to accentuate the
height when you stand on
the top, it is every bit as
beautiful as the canyon in
which it sits. And that, believe
me, is saying something.

AT 726 FEET HIGH, 660 FEET THICK AT THE BASE AND MORE THAN 1,200 FEET ACROSS, IT WAS EASILY THE LARGEST DAM IN THE WORLD.

It was one of these intake pipes that claimed the Hoover's final victim. On 20 December 1935 Patrick Tierney fell inside and died . . . exactly thirteen years after the first accident at the site claimed the life of his father.

Today there are other dams on the Colorado, and other reservoirs. And so great is the evaporation from these giant inland seas that by the time the Colorado reaches the coast in Mexico it's just a saline trickle. It hasn't just been beaten. Thanks to America's insatiable appetite for everything it's been killed.

Elsewhere in the US and the rest of the world there are other dams that dwarf the Hoover. But for me, it's still the most special, partly because of the 107 men who died making it and partly because of where it is.

There's something strangely odd about a straight, man-made edge in this barren and craggy terrain. It's as out of place as a footprint on the moon or the rusting hulk of the *Titanic* on the seabed. It shouldn't belong, and yet, somehow, it does.

I love it too for what it has created. Quite simply, without the Hoover Dam there would be no Las Vegas and no Phoenix. Without manageable water supplies and electricity these places could never have become the sprawling cities that they are today.

It's clean electricity too. To produce the 2,000 megawatts that comes out of the huge white wall every year would normally take 10,000 barrels of oil. And, of course, with oil you don't produce enough water as a by-product for 18 million people.

But the best thing about the Hoover Dam is the way it looks. With its art deco intake towers and that preposterous slope, which seems to accentuate the height when you stand on the top, it is every bit as beautiful as the canyon in which it sits. And that, believe me, is saying something.

It's regarded now as one of the prime terrorist targets in the world and as a result all commercial traffic and any bus carrying luggage is banned from driving over it. There's a fear that if it were to be destroyed, it would take a huge chunk of western America with it.

That would be sad, I'm sure. But not as sad as losing the dam. That would be unbearable.

AIRCRAFT CARRIER

It's a ship, first and foremost. But it's also a nuclear power station. And it's an airport. And it's an instrument of war. And above all this, it's city with shops, cinemas, hairdressers, banks, hospitals, its own television station, its own daily newspaper and 5,000 inhabitants.

Think about that. Would they put a nuclear reactor in the middle of a city? And would they let fighter jets land on the roof, when the whole thing is pitching and rolling in 50-foot seas? Because that's what happens on an aircraft carrier. They land F-14s and F-18s, which may be carrying nuclear weapons, on a nuclear power station in bad weather. Dangerous? Oh yes, which is why, when an invitation came to spend a couple of days on board the USS *Dwight D. Eisenhower*, I was off like a scalded rabbit.

Of course I imagined that I'd be landing in one of those F-14s, but no. They loaded me onto a propeller-driven cargo plane – they call it a Cod but it looks more like a toaster – and flew me out into the middle of the Atlantic to rendezvous with the mighty Nimitz Class carrier.

From the air it doesn't look mighty at all. In that vast grey ocean under a featureless grey sky it looks like a playing card. I know runways. I spend my life tearing up and down them in fast cars. So I know how long they have to be, and the one on top of the *Eisenhower* wasn't long enough. Not by a long way.

Here's what I knew was going to happen. We'd land, fail to stop, fall off the front and then the huge ship would run over the plane, turning it over and over until it, me and everyone else on board was minced by one of the three nuclear-powered, five-bladed propellers, each of which is 21 feet in diameter.

The closest I'd come to dying until this point was in a thunderstorm over Cuba. The Russian plane, which had been made in the fifties and used by the Angolan Air Force until it arrived in Cuba, was barely capable of flight in good conditions. But in a tropical storm it was quite literally upside down. And I remember thinking, 'Well, at least the kids can say that Dad went west in a Soviet fighter in the Caribbean.' It'd look good in the obituaries as well.

The impending landing on the *Eisenhower* was stirring up those memories. 'Yup, Dad died when he was liquidised by an aircraft carrier.' It had a ring.

As we descended the ship grew larger and larger in the plane's window, but it was still nowhere near large enough when we touched down, hooked up the arrester wire and went from 120 to zero mph in 0.0000000008 of a second.

Interestingly, my spleen, heart, lungs and liver continued to do 120 until they slammed into my ribcage whereupon they bounced back into place. Happily, you don't feel this because you're busy feeling around under the seat in front for both your eyeballs.

Moments later I was unbuckled and led onto the flight deck, where the jets did their best to blast me over the side and into the oggin. They say that working on the flight deck of a carrier is the most dangerous job in the world. I don't know about that but I can testify that it's certainly the noisiest.

And one of the least well organised. You'd imagine in a modern carrier that all of the flight operations would be computerised but, in fact, each of the planes is represented in air traffic control by a lump of wood which is pushed around a board by a man with no high-school qualifications. And this was the most high-tech thing I was to see for two days.

I was shown to my quarters, which were more like sixteenths. There was a bed that was one foot shorter than me and steel walls, a steel ceiling and a steel floor. There was no window, but then there is no window in any room on a carrier. You go on board and for months you have no idea whether it's day or night.

Certainly, the flight operations give no clue. I got no sleep at all on the first night, partly because it turned out my bed was steel too and partly because I seemed to have been given a room right underneath the steam catapult, which went off every twenty minutes or so.

And in between each firing an American came over the ship's PA system to announce at the top of his substantial, sergeant-major voice something important like: 'The donut-vending machine on Deck B

Here's what I knew was going to happen. We'd land, fail to stop, fall off the front and then the huge ship would run over the plane, turning it over and over until it, me and everyone else on board was minced by one of the three nuclear-powered, five-bladed propellers, each of which is 21 feet in diameter.

is now fully functional. We would like to thank the brave men
and women of the USS *Dwight D. Eisenhower* who have worked
so tirelessly to repair this invaluable equipment.'

In fact it turned out my room was nowhere near the steam
catapult. I know this because the following morning I went to look
at it and it took nigh on half an hour to get there. Then it took a
further 90 minutes to get to the arrester-wire control room.

This was amazing. I just thought the wire was a piece of elastic
but it's a steel cable that's connected to a hydraulic jack. And before
a plane can land, someone on the flight deck has to telephone
the man in the arrester wire room to tell him what sort it is.

A big heavy F-14 needs a different setting than a Cod, for
instance. Seems sensible, expect for two things. First of all, the
arrester-wire room is the noisiest place on earth – you couldn't
even hear the million-watt PA system in there – leave alone what
someone in the other end of a phone was saying. And secondly,
the man who had to set the machine was easily the stupidest
person I'd ever met.

Had I known when I was coming into land in the Cod that my life
was in the hands of a man who could neither hear nor string two
words together, I'd have jumped.

I asked him a few questions. A few of his spots burst. And I set
off on a brief two-hour walk to find the admiral. At one point I thought
I recognised one of the corridors. It seemed to be a slightly less-dark
shade of grey, but actually my perception was ebbing, along with
my will to live.

Life on the bridge was much better. It has windows from which
you can see the flotilla a carrier needs when it's at sea. There's the
fuel tanker, for the planes stoopid (the *Eisenhower* has enough juice
in its reactors to last a million miles). And then there's the food ship,
which, being American, was huge. The *Eisenhower*'s crew get through
18,000 meals a day, which means they need 5,000 gallons of milk
a week and, in a typical cruise, 160,000 eggs.

That's before you start to feed the crews on the smaller warships
that tag along to protect the big daddy (and the food ship) from

THE *EISENHOWER*'S CREW GET THROUGH 18,000 MEALS A DAY, WHICH MEANS THEY NEED 5,000 GALLONS OF MILK A WEEK AND, IN A TYPICAL CRUISE, 160,000 EGGS.

a waterborne assault, and the sub, to protect it from beneath. There were fourteen ships out there, all to take care of the carrier.

And yet, should the balloon go up, the *Eisenhower* would leave its escorts far behind. A good modern warship can thunder along at 28 or 29 knots. But a Nimitz Class carrier will hammer along at 33. It is, according to the admiral, the racing car of the seas.

But it's the size of these extraordinary ships that boggles the mind most of all. Of course, there are longer oil tankers plodding around the seaways, but in terms of sheer bulk the Nimitz Class carriers are right out in a class of their own. They weigh as near as makes no difference 100,000 tons. Their turbines produce 280,000 horsepower. And the nuclear power on board allows continuous operation for fifteen years. To power a normal carrier for that long would take 11 billion barrels of fuel oil.

And now we're starting to get into the serious statistics that arouse the hairs on the back of your neck. The *Eisenhower* is as tall as a 24-storey building, she can carry up to 90 planes and she costs £300 million a year to run. Mind you, that's small fry compared to the £3 BILLION she cost to build. And remember, America has twelve of these monsters.

The idea behind them is very simple. They turn up off the enemy coast and Johnny Foreigner is so cowed by their enormity he lays

It's the size of these extraordinary ships that boggles the mind most of all. Of course, there are longer oil tankers plodding around the seaways, but in terms of sheer bulk the Nimitz Class carriers are right out in a class of their own.

The 100,000-ton USS *John C. Stennis* Nimitz
Class carrier steams along beside the 20,000-
ton British aircraft carrier HMS *Invincible*.

down his assault rifle and opens a shop. Quite how that'll work when
the latest big carrier takes to the seas, I don't know. You see, it's called
the USS *Ronald Reagan*.

Whatever, the *Eisenhower* was certainly scary. Not because of the
nukes it can rain down on your hometown but because I'd gone to the
loo and was lost. I asked for directions many times, but it turned out
the man in the arrester-wire room had been given the Big Job because
he was the brightest man on board. Most didn't seem to have heard of
the bridge or the admiral and they certainly didn't know where he or
it might be.

Then they sounded general quarters, which is a bit like the teacher
turning round. Everyone with a proper job must rush to battle stations
and everyone in an ancillary capacity has to stay wherever they are,
behind locked-down bulkheads. I was in a steel room with a steel floor
and a steel ceiling. It could have been my bedroom. But because I fell
asleep in there, it seemed unlikely.

Eventually, when the two-hour general quarters was over, a search
party found me and from that point on I was given a minder. I forget his
name but I do recall that he looked like Barney Rubble, and he really
was the daftest man on board.

'Attention!' screamed the intercom, and I immediately put my
fingers in my ears assuming another donut machine had been
mended. But no. It turned out an F-14 was on its final approach . . .
and one of its engines was on fire.

'Quick,' I said to Barney. 'We must get up to the Vulture's Nest
so that my crew can film the fighter pilot nursing his stricken plane
onto the deck.'

Barney agreed but seemed more bothered about getting our room
account settled. Amazingly, visitors to the carrier are charged $8
a night. 'Here,' I said plunging a ten into his podgy hands. But it was
no good. Barney needed to give me change but didn't have any. 'OK,'
I yelled. 'Here's a fifty. That'll cover all of us.' And turned to run.

Barney wasn't sure. So he pulled out a pencil and started to do
some sums. 'Let's see,' he mumbled to himself, 'eight dollars a room
and there are six of them. That's six times eight which is, er, um . . .'

Pretty soon he ran out of fingers so he assembled a selection of alternatives before working out, after a full ten minutes, that the answer was 48.

'Well,' he said with a smile. 'We're no further on. I still owe you two dollars and I still don't have any change.' He wouldn't keep it and as a result we missed the spectacle of a mono-engined F-14 thudding onto the carrier's deck. Thanks Barney. 'Don't mention it,' he said cheerily.

And then it was time to go home. We were loaded back into the toaster and, to my enormous surprise, wheeled right to the front of the ship, giving us no runway at all to use for the take off. We'd simply be attached to the steam catapult, which would fling us off the end, after which we'd fall into the sea and be minced by the props.

We were told not to worry by the grinning Barney, who said the steam catapult could fire a VW Beetle seventeen miles. So it'd have no problem with our little Cod, especially as the ship points into wind for every take-off. Every little detail of the launch procedure was discussed in fact . . . except one.

So, the 100,000-ton ship turned into the wind. Our pilot wound up his little engines to full power. The deck hands made all sorts of silly *Top Gun* hand signals and, with a savagery that's hard to explain in print, we were off.

Immediately there was a resounding crack and I knew something had broken. Sure enough, the plane dipped as it cleared the end of the runway and I braced myself for the impact that never came.

It turned out that the steel ingot that is used to attach the nose wheel to the catapult is designed to break, with a crack, as the plane lifts off. It sounds catastrophic but Barney, bless him, had forgotten to mention it.

My two days on that carrier were, without any question or shadow of doubt, the noisiest, most uncomfortable, most depressing I've ever endured. I was startled by the average IQ of those I met and genuinely amazed at the conditions in which they live. There was no drink on board, sex was not allowed and the smoking quarters were barbaric.

And yet the ship itself was a wondrous piece of engineering. Sure, it was designed to attack without pity and rain fire without remorse. But there's no doubt that beneath its nuclear heart it has a soul.

ALFA ROMEO 166

By any logical standard the Alfa Romeo 166 is not a very good car. Compared to, say, a 5-series BMW, it is not especially fast, spacious, economical or well equipped, and it doesn't handle terribly well either.

It is pulled along by its front wheels, and while this space-saving option works well on small hatchbacks it's rarely satisfactory in a large saloon. The problem is that the front wheels have enough to do dealing with the steering. To entrust them with the power from a 3.2-litre V6 engine as well is a recipe for disaster.

If you apply too much throttle in a corner in a rear-wheel-drive car, it is, of course, the rear wheels that lose traction. The back end consequently swings round and you know exactly what you do about that because you were told by your driving instructor. You steer into the skid, and all is well.

Get it wrong and the news is still good because the back will swing all the way round and you'll go backwards into a tree. This is fine. It means your death is as instant as it is unexpected.

In a front-wheel-drive car it is the front wheels that lose traction, which means you can do whatever you like with the steering wheel – it won't make a jot of difference. You'll hit the tree and, to make matters worse, you'll see it coming . . .

But there are problems with front-wheel drive long before you get to a corner. I'm talking about torque steer. When you put your foot down, hard, the steering wheel squirms this way and that, as the power applies all kinds of unpleasant and unnatural forces to wheels that, by their very nature, aren't bolted in place.

Alfa uses front-wheel drive because it's cheap. And there's a 'win free save' feel to the cockpit as well. In a BMW these days you get a little pinprick of light from the rear-view mirror that bathes all the controls in a puddle of red light. You also get cup holders and volume controls for the stereo on the steering wheel. None of this expensive-to-design stuff is available on a 166.

As a result, anyone with £30,000 to spend on a large executive saloon car is going to be swayed by the Beemer, and as a result of that, Alfa Romeo's sales in Britain are what an economist would call 'pitiful'.

THE POOR SOD WHO BUYS ONE NEW, FOR £30,000, WILL LOSE £17,000 IN A YEAR. IT'LL COST HIM £50 A DAY BEFORE HE'S PUT ANY FUEL IN THE TANK OR COUGHED UP FOR SOME INSURANCE.

To make matters worse, no one wants them second-hand either, which means the poor sod who did buy one new, for £30,000, will lose £17,000 in a year. So he ends up with a car that's not as fast, not as well equipped and not as nice to drive as a BMW. And what's more, it'll cost him £50 a day before he's put any fuel in the tank or coughed up for some insurance. Frankly, then, anyone who buys a 166 is a full-on window-licking mentalist.

And yet, if I were in the market for a businessman's car, I'd have one like a shot.

Don't worry. This has nothing to do with Alfas of old being driven by men on black-and-white round racetracks that don't exist any more. Buying a car because the firm that makes it used to be amazing 50 years ago would be like employing a team of Italian builders because the Romans were so organised. It's people who make a car what it is, and the people who made Alfas so strong in Grand Prix racing in the fifties are all either dead or sitting in wingback chairs, drooling.

The people who run Alfa Romeo today are Fiat, and the people who run Fiat spend most of their days looking at the accounts, groaning.

As a place to be the 166 has no equal. It's a combination, really, of the hand-stitched upholstery and the exquisite choice of colours. Black carpets. Tan seats. Why does no one else do that?

It's as European and as perfect as a girl in a little black dress, at a pavement café, sipping an espresso coffee. You have a 166. You have style.

However, they are for the most part Italian, which means that they have a certain exuberance and a definite sense of style, and that shows. The 166 may not be very good as a car, but as a place to be it has no equal. It's a combination, really, of the hand-stitched upholstery and the exquisite choice of colours. Black carpets. Tan seats. Why does no one else do that?

And look at the styling. Some say the headlights are a bit piggy and the nose is far too big but that's like chucking Cindy Crawford out of bed because she has a mole.

Ignore the details and concentrate on the overall shape, the stance. Note the way it seems to be leaning forward, like it's in a hurry. And note too the gracefulness of the lines as they flow from the back to the front. This is an extraordinarily beautiful car. And, if you go for navy-blue paint, elegant and cool too.

I can see BMWs and Jaguars parked outside the local golf club. I can see Mercs parked outside celebrity parties, waiting to take the drunken *Brookside* star home. An Alfa though? I can see that parked outside an embassy cocktail party, at a schloss, in Austria. It's as European and as perfect as a girl in a little black dress, at a pavement café, sipping an espresso coffee. You have a 166. You have style.

And then there's the driving experience. Yes, it's all a bit wayward when you're going for it, but when you're not – and let's be honest, for 99 per cent of the time you won't be – there's always a sense that you're in a car. There's a crackle from the exhaust and a muted howl from the engine. You feel the road through the seat of your pants and when you run over a white line you can tell through the feel of the wheel whether it was gloss paint or emulsion.

Most modern executive cars try to distance you from all of this. You get in, move a couple of controls and with no fuss at all you arrive at your destination. The 166 doesn't do that. It lets you know, always, that you're in a car. It makes you feel like the organic part of a machine. That, I'm sure, would be a nuisance if you're a motorist.

But if you're a driver, it is exactly what you want.

BLACKBIRD

In the mid sixties an RAF fighter pilot was cruising down the east coast of England in his Lightning when he saw something unusual. 'It looked exactly like one of those sci-fi Airfix kits that I'd had as a boy in the fifties,' he told me, years later.

Opening the taps a little on his fighter, he came up behind the mysterious plane for a better look. The USAF markings identified it as friendly so he pulled alongside to wave at the pilot. But he never got the chance because when the Americans saw him coming: whoomph. With an explosion of noise, they, and their astonishing machine, were gone. 'I simply could not believe how fast it was,' he said.

Back at base his colleagues were sceptical. 'I see,' they said, 'so you saw a huge black plane that spewed circular blue flame out of its engines and rocketed away so quickly you couldn't keep up.' It did sound absurd because, at the time, everyone knew, with absolute certainty, that just about the fastest plane in the sky was the Lightning.

Everyone was wrong. Because what the RAF pilot had seen was the SR-71. The Blackbird. And it wasn't just the fastest plane in the world then. It's the fastest plane in the world now too.

At the time it was top secret, only taking off and landing when it was dark. And the reason why those Americans never saw our friend coming until he was alongside is that it flew with everything turned off. A black shadow in the sky. A streak that left almost no electronic mumbo-jumbo in its wake. It had the same radar signature as a fruit fly.

This was a plane built for spying. It carried no missiles and no guns. Its job was to climb, at enormous speed, to a height of 90,000 feet, from where it was neither visible nor audible to anyone on earth. 90,000 feet is 17 miles. It's 60,000 feet higher than a commercial jetliner goes. It's 30,000 feet higher than Concorde flew. Any more and its mighty ram-jet engines would be sucking on the vacuum of space.

Once there, in a world it could truly call its own, it would go even faster, moving up past 2,000 mph to three times the speed of sound. And from that far up, at that kind of velocity, its ability to cover ground was staggering. In just one hour it could survey 100,000 square miles of the earth's surface.

FLYING AT 90,000 FEET, IT WAS NEITHER VISIBLE NOR AUDIBLE TO ANYONE ON EARTH. 90,000 FEET IS 17 MILES. IT'S 60,000 FEET HIGHER THAN A COMMERCIAL JETLINER GOES. IT'S 30,000 FEET HIGHER THAN CONCORDE FLEW.

And it was almost completely unshootdownable. I spoke once to one of its pilots, who said that if by some miracle he was detected in enemy air space, he still had absolutely nothing to fear. 'We'd see the MiGs coming up to get us, but when they hit 60,000 feet we'd have gone and they would fall out of the sky.'

Even if a MiG could get itself in front of the Blackbird and fire off a missile, there was almost no chance of a hit. 'Think about it,' said the pilot. 'The missile's going at Mach 2. We're doing Mach 3. That's a closing speed of five times the speed of sound and no computer at that time could have worked things out fast enough. Believe me, we were up there with complete impunity.'

The key to this height and speed – speed that saw a Blackbird once get from New York to London in just under 1 hour and 55 minutes, including a spot of in-flight refuelling – is its power.

The figures the engines produce are as vast as they are meaningless. But there is one that gives pause for thought. Flat out, just 20 per cent of the thrust is produced by the basic engines themselves. 80 per cent, then, is coming from nowhere at all. So how is this possible?

The Blackbird was almost completely
unshootdownable. I spoke once to one of
its pilots, who said that if by some miracle
he was detected in enemy air space, he still
had absolutely nothing to fear. 'We'd see
the MiGs coming up to get us, but when
they hit 60,000 feet we'd have gone
and they would fall out of the sky.'

Well, in essence, those big pointy things that stick out of the intakes steer most of the air into escape channels that never go anywhere near the blades. This air is simply compressed and then, as it gets to the exhaust, ignited. And the more air you push in, the more thrust you get.

In other words the jet gets you up to a certain speed, but from that point onwards there are no moving parts. You simply burn the air and watch the speedo climb. Quite literally, the faster you go the faster it goes.

It may be simple but the spectacle that results is heavenly. On full throttle, two giant blue plumes are left in the Blackbird's wake, each framing a series of perfect blue balls of equally perfect energy. You watch it and you think, 'God almighty. How did man ever create a sight like that?' And then you think, 'Crikey. It's all very well making power like that but how, in the name of all that's holy, do we tame it?'

The simple answer is, we don't. Occasionally one of these engines will suffer from what the pilots call an unstart. You'll be flying along when it will suddenly 'burp', ejecting air not from the back but from the front. This is bad news, because all of a sudden you have full thrust from one side of the plane and full drag from the other. The result is a spin, and the result of that is a quiet and undignified end for the two men on board. Quiet because the crash won't be reported – how can a plane crash if it officially 'doesn't exist'? – and undignified because when you hit the ground in an SR-71 they don't bury the remains so much as hose them into the nearest drain.

Apparently, before an unstart there are tiny, audible warnings that you can just about hear if you're really concentrating. But this makes the Blackbird not very relaxing. You have to keep your ears open, constantly, for the slightest hint that one of the jets is about to break wind. And you then have to think what you might do about it . . .

When the second Blackbird ever made crashed in Utah in 1963 two farmers who arrived on the scene were told by the military personnel that the plane had been carrying atomic bombs. This was a lie but word got round, and as a result none of the locals turned up to poke around in the wreckage. The press was later told that the locals had got their wires crossed, that there were no nukes on board and that

A BLACKBIRD ONCE FLEW FROM NEW YORK TO LONDON IN JUST UNDER 1 HOUR AND 55 MINUTES, AND THAT INCLUDED SLOWING DOWN FOR A SPOT OF IN-FLIGHT REFUELLING.

the plane was an F-105 Thunderchief. That was another lie, but it's how the accident is still catalogued today.

Of the 40 Blackbirds made, 20 have crashed, killing all sorts of Lockheed engineers and CIA operatives who were sitting in the back. But amazingly, when you think of the speed they're going when they bale out, not a single USAF pilot has ever died at the wheel.

Perhaps the most astonishing crash happened in 1966, when it was decided the SR-71 would make an ideal launch platform for a new kind of reconnaissance drone. This pilotless jet would be launched from a mounting platform on the Blackbird's back. Brilliant. Except for two things.

Why fit a supplementary spying device on the back of what was already the perfect espionage tool? And how was this 'mini Blackbird' supposed to penetrate the ferocious shockwave coming from the mother ship's nose? No one seemed to have thought about that. And no one did until the drone took off and ran slap bang into what may as well have been a wall.

Unable to get through, the pilotless aircraft dived and smacked straight into the Blackbird, cutting it clean in half.

On full throttle, two giant
blue plumes are left in the
Blackbird's wake, each
framing a series of perfect
blue balls of equally perfect
energy. You watch it and
you think, 'God almighty.
How did man ever create
a sight like that?'

Both crew members survived the impact, and both survived the ejection and parachute descent, but one, Ray Torrick, died when he landed in the Pacific Ocean and opened his visor. His pressure suit promptly filled with water and he was drowned.

This is very sad, and yet it pales into insignificance alongside the destruction of the SR-71. That makes me angry. How could they have let this drone, this bastard infant son, turn on its mother? What were they thinking of?

I hate to think of a crashed Blackbird. It causes me physical pain. Because I've actually been to its natural breeding ground, Edwards Air Force Base, in the high desert of California, and let me tell you: this is so much more than a collection of exotic materials paid for by a paranoid nation and designed in an overgrown schoolboy's wet dream. The SR-71 feels, looks and, most importantly of all, *sounds* like it's alive.

When I walked though the door of its hangar the first thing to take me by surprise was the size of its engines. They're actually wider than the fuselage of the plane. The second shock was the feel of the titanium airframe. Even in the chill of a desert night, it felt warm and soft to the touch; not at all like metal. More like moleskin, in fact.

But the most eerie sensation was the noise. When a Blackbird flies the friction is so massive, and generates so much heat, that the whole plane grows by a foot. Then, after it lands and begins to cool, it shrinks back down again.

The plane I was pawing had not flown for six months but you could still hear it creaking and groaning. And there was a constant drip-drip-drip as its oils and fuel leaked out of the tanks, their seams distorted by the shrinkage.

The nose, however, would never go back to its original shape. After two hours at 2,250 mph it became all wrinkled, and the ground crew would have to smooth it into shape again using blowtorches. It was, said one pilot, like ironing a shirt.

Inside the tiny cockpit it is mind-boggling. You have, oh, about 2,000 dials, none of which is a speedometer, and, because this was designed when the world thought blenders were space age, there are no computer screens. You have a sense that all is mechanical in there, rather than electronic. And that helps reinforce the sense of Blackbird being a living, breathing being.

No computer has a soul. You have no sense that a wire and a microchip are alive because they don't actually do anything. But when you pull a lever and hydraulic fluid causes a part to actually move, that's different. And that's what happens in the Blackbird, a product of the fifties that could still cut it right up to the last ever flight in 1999.

This was the most successful spying device ever. In the early days the U-2 was too slow, and too low. Gary Powers would testify to that, since his was shot down by a surface-to-air missile in 1960. Worse still, he failed to activate the self-destruct button and, when captured, he was disinclined to swallow his cyanide pill. Maybe the Russians learned something from him. Maybe they didn't, but either way, two years later another U-2 was shot down, and the pilot killed, over Cuba, right in the middle of the missile crisis.

Shortly after that the space race began, but early satellites were no match for planes. They had physically to drop a film canister back to earth, which would have to be retrieved and sent to Boots. Only when it was learned how to watch 'real time' footage did these eyes in space start to make sense. But they've rather lost the point in the modern age.

They were fine when Russia was the bad guy, but where do you put them now? Over Iraq? Iran? Syria? Libya? Afghanistan? You can never tell where the trouble will come from next. And it's the devil's own job to move one.

The Blackbird would solve all that. It can go wherever it wants, taking as many pictures as it wants, of whatever takes its fancy. It was the perfect solution in 1966, and nothing's changed.

SUBMARINE

Were there to be a war tomorrow, a big one against a properly tooled-up country, I wouldn't hesitate for a second. I'd buy myself a nice white polo-neck jumper, get on the first train to Scotland and join the submarine service.

The infantry requires far too much running around, the cavalry spends most of its time playing polo, which is no good because I like horses when they're accompanied with chips but not when they have saddles, and the air force is just plain dangerous. That means it'd have to be the navy and since I get seasick watching naval battles on television, I'd need a posting in subs.

There are other advantages to submarines too. Like if the balloon were to go up, I'd sneak off to a Pacific Island somewhere, park the boat under an overhanging palm tree where it couldn't be seen by nosy satellites and spend the war drinking rum punches with exotic girls called Miu Miu.

Then when the fighting was over I'd shoot a few pretend bullet holes in the hull and sail home, claiming that my suntan was down to a faulty reactor.

This plan assumes that I'd be the captain but that, I'm afraid, is a given. I couldn't possibly join the crew of a sub as an enlisted man. They have to share beds, which is suspect, but worse, they have to crap in public, and I'm sorry but I can't do that. I need my own lavatory, with lots of reading material, in a part of the ship where I can be alone. So, it's captain or nothing.

Actually, I've always loved submarines. Way back when I was a small boy my uncle, who lived in Nova Scotia and claimed to be a salesman, once came from Canada to England on a sub. He never said why or what it was like, but I spent the next ten years hanging on to his trouser leg. To me, he was James Bond. He probably was.

Secrecy is the biggest appeal of the submarine; its ability to wage a sneaky war. When the idea was first seriously mooted for an underwater vessel, the Royal Navy's top brass, which is fuelled by money and tradition in equal parts, dismissed the idea as 'underhand and ungentlemanly'.

It might also have had something to do with the fact that the first real submarine, with an engine, was designed by a British chap . . . who had strong Irish Republican sympathies.

Mostly though, they really didn't like the idea of a ship attacking another ship without showing itself first. That would be like having a duel with one of the contestants hiding in a hedge. Me, though, I love the idea of creeping up to a target, blowing it to kingdom come and then slipping away without leaving so much as a ripple. It seems safe, somehow, and better still, it's a job you can do sitting down. Of course, the captain (me) has to stand occasionally, but at least there's a handy periscope to lean on.

It was not always thus.

We've read Nicholas Monserrat, we know about the WW2 convoys and how countless million tons of ships were sunk each year, and we're told of Churchill's concerns about the U-boat. 'The only thing that ever frightened me during the war was the U-boat peril,' he wrote in his memoirs.

In the First World War the German subs could be contained by mining the English Channel off Dover. But in the Second World War Germany conquered France, which allowed them to station their subs on the Atlantic coast. This meant the convoys coming from America were within easy reach, as were any ships going to the Med or the furthest-flung corners of the Empire.

Beating the threat became a question of mathematics. To many it sounded silly, grouping all the ships together in one lump for the voyage from the USA to the UK. Surely, the sceptics reasoned, if a convoy is discovered by a U-boat, it can pick off the lot, whereas if it happens across just one ship on its own, that's bad but not catastrophic.

True, but when a sub finds a ship it must manoeuvre itself into the right position, something that's not always possible. If it were to fail with one ship, it wouldn't have to wait that long before another trundled by. If it were to fail after sighting a convoy, it would miss all the ships in it, and it might be days before it happened upon another.

Put simply, in the time it had at sea, a sub could not sink any more

U-boat design was beaten by technology. Consider the old game of paper, scissors and stone. The sub can beat the ship, but as soon as it surfaces for air or fuel it's always going to be beaten by the plane. And the U-boats had to surface . . .

convoy ships than it would have done had it been presented with
a series of individual targets.

And what's more, because the convoys always had warships
to escort them, it meant the U-boats were being drawn to the Royal
Navy's guns. To get at the merchantmen, the Germans had to get
past the destroyers first and that was never easy.

Convoys forced the Nazis to rethink their battle plans. They spread
their subs out in a chain across the Atlantic, and then when a convoy
was sighted messages were flashed to the base in France and other
subs were zeroed in on the position. We had the convoys. They had
the wolf packs. But the battle was actually fought in laboratories
and workshops back at home.

We developed sonar. They developed techniques for evading it.
We made depth charges that could sink to 500 feet before exploding.
They built pressure hulls that could go deeper still. We made fast
frigates to catch an escaping sub. They made more powerful engines.
We cracked their codes. They cracked ours. We developed radar that
could be fitted to aircraft. They developed a radar detector so a sub
could dive before the plane got there. We introduced four-engined
bombers that could offer protection over the whole Atlantic. They
developed snorkels for the diesel engines so they could stay
submerged. It was a constant battle of the brains, and they were
very good. But in the end they didn't starve Britain into submission.
Because we were better.

The U-boat peril may have scared Churchill to death and it may
have caused countless thousand utterly miserable deaths. There
were times too, especially in 1941 and parts of 1942, when a small
fleet of German subs really did have the upper hand over the largest
merchant fleet and the most powerful navy in the world.

At the start of the war we had 3,000 merchant ships and the
Germans 100 U-boats, only six of which were in the Atlantic at any one
time. Yet with just six boats, the Nazis sank 400 ships in the first eight
months. They were blowing them up twice as fast as we could replace
them. And by the summer of 1941 the Germans had twelve U-boats at

AT THE START OF THE WAR WE HAD 3,000 MERCHANT SHIPS AND THE GERMANS 100 U-BOATS, ONLY SIX OF WHICH WERE IN THE ATLANTIC AT ANY ONE TIME. YET WITH JUST SIX BOATS, THE NAZIS SANK 400 SHIPS IN THE FIRST EIGHT MONTHS.

sea. They were aiming to have 300 out there, and that really would have been that.

But in the end the old U-boat design was beaten by technology. Consider the old game of paper, scissors and stone. The sub can beat the ship, but as soon as it surfaces for air or fuel it's always going to be beaten by the plane. And the U-boats had to surface . . .

But then came the dawn of nuclear power, and submarines that could stay down there, making no noise at all, for month after month after month. If Churchill thought those old German diesel boats were frightening, then he would have been utterly terrified by the nukes.

Not only could this all-new weapon beat the paper, the scissors and the rock but also cruisers and aircraft carriers, and when the inter-continental ballistic missile was developed, whole countries as well.

The job of these dedicated missile boats is to pootle about, like mice in carpet slippers, with their ballistic missiles, waiting for an order to destroy an entire continent.

It could be argued, so I will, that if Britain's MoD really were a Ministry of *Defence*, then it could dispense with the army and the air force. All it would need to protect us is one of these 'boomers'.

When the Argentine light-cruiser *Belgrano* was hit by two torpedoes from the snout of *Conqueror*, a British hunter-killer, the enemy escort ships immediately gave chase. They were out of ideas after just five miles. The Royal Navy vessel had approached unseen, fired unseen and simply disappeared. After the conflict was over *Conqueror* sailed into Scottish waters flying the Jolly Roger.

The job of the dedicated missile boats is to pootle about, like mice in carpet slippers, with their ballistic missiles, waiting for an order to destroy an entire continent.

No really. If anyone was going to going to attack, they'd try to remove our nuclear capability first – but how do you do that when you have no clue where it is?

Finding one of these things is not like looking for a needle in a haystack. Because a haystack is small. A boomer is huge, for sure – the Russian Typhoons are as big as First World War battleships – but they can hide anywhere in two-thirds of the world's surface. One could be sitting a mile off your coast, or it could be under the polar ice cap. It could be anywhere.

Once I saw one of these things surface, quite unexpectedly, in the Channel. One minute the sea was calm and blue and seemingly full of nothing more dangerous than cod. And then the next a huge black shape, the most menacing thing I'd ever seen, was just . . . there.

It made me feel safe. It was a reminder that, despite all of Britain's woes and insecurities, we're still one of the world's big players. Today you really can judge a country on whether it has a fleet of nuclear subs. Such a thing is a defining characteristic, a measure of technical clout. It means we can walk a little taller.

But actually, my favourite of all the submarines ever made are the hunter-killers, the super-fast attack boats that prowl the seas in search of the boomers.

A modern nuclear-powered American Los Angeles Class submarine can dive to 1,500 feet. It can reach 20 knots on the surface, which means you could water-ski behind it, and, more impressively, 35 knots when it's submerged. It can fire torpedoes at shipping or, if ordered to do so by the president, cruise missiles at cities several hundred miles away. It is like the Alien – a perfect killing machine.

And how do you destroy such a thing? It is so fast and so manoeuvrable that by the time you've found it it's somewhere else. You're aiming your depth charges or your torpedoes at something that simply isn't there any more.

To give you an idea of how quiet these subs are, an American boat once trailed a Soviet boomer for 40 days without being detected. Imagine having a shadow for nearly six weeks and not knowing.

In fact in the Cold War the only time you really knew you had a hunter-killer up your jacksie was when it rammed you by mistake. Since 1967 there have been eleven collisions between Russian, American and British subs. One British boat came back to port with the bow scoured by a Russian propeller.

Happily, however, a nuclear submarine has only fired its torpedoes in anger once. Needless to say, it was one of ours, after the Argies invaded Mrs Thatcher.

When the Argentine light-cruiser *Belgrano* was hit by two torpedoes from the snout of *Conqueror*, a British hunter-killer, the enemy escort ships immediately gave chase. They were out of ideas after just five miles. The Royal Navy vessel had approached unseen, fired unseen and simply disappeared.

Underhand and ungentlemanly perhaps. But at least the sub's commanding officer, Chris Wreford-Brown, maintained all the finest Navy traditions of understatement when asked about the incident later. 'The Royal Navy spent thirteen years preparing me for such an occasion,' he said. 'It would have been regarded as extremely dreary if I had fouled it up.'

He didn't, and as a result the rest of the Argentine Navy returned to port where it stayed for the remainder of the war. Fighting the bits of the Royal Navy that could be seen was going to be hard enough. Fighting the bits that were invisible – that would be impossible.

After the conflict was over *Conqueror* sailed into Scottish waters flying the Jolly Roger, a sign that she'd had a kill while on tour. But despite her place in the history books she was decommissioned in 1990. Her periscope was given to a museum and today she sits in Faslane, quietly rotting.

SPACE SHUTTLE

We expect astronauts to have balls the size of Corvettes and a Readybrek glow of invincibility. We expect them to be a bit like superheroes only a little more super and a lot more heroic. We expect them to be nothing like anyone we've ever met before.

When I arranged to meet one a few years ago I was expecting a blend of Robert Plant and Batman to barge through the door, but what I got was Hoot Gibson, who had beige trousers, a bad shirt, a Toyota Camry and a much-publicised fondness for the music of the Moody Blues.

As the day wore on I realised why you should never judge a book by its cover, or by the tunes it plays in its four-door saloon. Hoot may have had a four-dollar haircut and enough man-made fibres in his shirt to keep the petrochemical industry going for a thousand years, but he can do stuff that better-dressed, better-paid men cannot. Like fly his homemade racing plane, upside down, under the blades of a hovering helicopter, or dive-bomb Vietnamese missile sites in his Phantom jet or, best of all, control the most powerful machine ever made by man . . . the Space Shuttle.

Like Hoot, it doesn't look like much in the pictures. It's a big ungainly lorry that lumbers off its launch pad for an invisible rendezvous in the inky blackness of space. Then it lands again. Wow. Big deal.

But then I was taken to the Louisiana facility where Rockwell makes and tests the engines for this delivery truck. The engineers had said I could stand 200 yards from the test bed but recommended I wore ear defenders. 'No thanks,' I said, with a patronising smile. 'I've seen The Who live five times. I know what noise is.' But not even Keith Moon had prepared me for the ferocity of that sound. It's a kind of white noise that you can feel as much as you hear. And it feels like the work of God.

It certainly messes with nature. When the test was over the massive exhaust cloud, which is nothing but water vapour, rose slowly into the heat of that sultry Louisiana afternoon. For a while it hung there, an incongruous white lump in the uninterrupted ocean of blue. And then it started to rain. NASA, it seems, is making its own weather.

The Shuttle has three of these engines but surprisingly, once you've seen the biblical power that just one produces, their combined thrust would not even lift the Shuttle two feet off the launch pad.

What they do when they're ignited, around six seconds before launch, is cause the whole machine, the Shuttle itself, its two solid rocket boosters and its fuel tank, to actually flex against the restraining bolts.

Eventually it can flex no more, and begins quite literally to 'boing' back the other way. By this stage the countdown is complete, and as the nose passes through the vertical the solid rocket boosters are ignited. Now the machine is producing 37 million horsepower and there are no restraining bolts on earth that could restrain that.

One astronaut described the Shuttle mounted on this tremendous power-delivery system as being like a butterfly mounted to a bullet.

On the television the Shuttle does seem to lumber off the launch pad, but 'lumber' is quite the wrong word. In fact by the time the tail has cleared the tower it's already doing 120 mph. 'It doesn't feel like it's lumbering from inside,' says Hoot. 'You just hear an enormous explosion and pray you're going up.'

Once the SRBs have been ignited they can only be turned off by one man. He sits in a little shed on the other side of the launch site. He has never met the astronauts on board and they have never met him. If something goes wrong and the Shuttle appears to be on a collision course with Miami, or any other population centre, his job is to push a little button on his desk. This sends a radio signal to two detonators that are linked to a strip of explosives. If you look carefully in the pictures, you can even see them, two long wavy yellow lines that run the length of each SRB. And then the Shuttle, along with everyone on board, will be blown up.

So far the anonymous man has never been used. But if you saw what happened to *Challenger* back in 1986, you know why he's there ... the Shuttle has not far short of the destructive power of an atomic bomb.

Obviously, by channelling this non-stop stream of power, the acceleration is vivid. Thirty seconds after leaving the launch pad the

Shuttle is going through the sound barrier and the world is being treated to two sonic booms – one from its nose and another from its tail.

Then, after two minutes, the empty SRBs are ejected and fall back into the Atlantic, from where they will be recovered and reused. If something were to go wrong at this point, the crew would simply point the nose at the earth again and land at an emergency runway that NASA maintains in Spain. The journey, a spectacular arc from Florida to the Iberian peninsular, would, according to Hoot, take 'less than twenty minutes'.

But if nothing goes wrong, the Shuttle continues to pick up speed thanks to its main engines. They're sucking fuel through a 17-inch-diameter pipe at such a rate that they'd drain an Olympic-sized swimming pool in ten seconds flat. After eight minutes they've used every one of the 500,000 gallons in the huge tank. And for this mission their work is done. The Space Shuttle is on the edge of space, doing 17,500 mph.

Truck? I don't think so.

But if you think getting to space is a bewildering array of big numbers, it's nothing compared with the complexities of getting back down again.

To penetrate the earth's atmosphere, the nose cone has to withstand a shockwave that, at 3,000 degrees Fahrenheit, is considerably hotter than the surface of the sun. Crew members sitting in the back seats of the upper deck can look backwards through the glass 'moon' roof and see nothing but a sheet of white-hot flame. And after they've barged their way through this the pilot has got to slow the machine down from 17,000 mph to a safe landing speed of 211 mph.

This is tricky, partly because he has no fuel left and therefore no power and partly because the Shuttle has the aerodynamic properties of an Aga. As a result, he has to make a series of sweeping turns, washing off speed with each one, but even then the rate of descent is still seven times greater than in a normal plane. Put it this way: if a crew member were to jump as the Shuttle was on its final approach, the plane would hit the ground before he did.

In space the crew take just the most astonishing photographs. There they are, fiddling about in their balloon suits, while far below we can see Italy sliding by.

THE SHUTTLE'S MAIN ENGINES SUCK FUEL THROUGH A 17-INCH-DIAMETER PIPE AT SUCH A RATE THAT THEY'D DRAIN AN OLYMPIC-SIZED SWIMMING POOL IN TEN SECONDS FLAT.

I love the Space Shuttle. I love the sense that every single figure and every single fact is more mind-boggling than the last.

When it's in space we know the crew take just the most astonishing photographs. There they are, fiddling about in their balloon suits, while far below we can see Italy sliding by. It's the juxtaposition, I think, of utter civilisation in the background and absolute hostility in the foreground that makes the shots so spectacular.

And it really is hostile where Hoot and his colleagues strut their stuff. For instance, if they fly with one side of the Shuttle facing the sun for too long, one cargo-door will swell and won't close properly. So then they have to turn the whole caboodle round to heat the other side up as well.

No astronaut has ever been lost in space but there have been close calls. The 46th mission called for the crew to launch a European satellite from the cargo area and then fly in formation while checks were carried out by staff at the command centre in Germany.

All was going well until someone on earth pushed the wrong button. Instead of rotating, the satellite veered off course and started heading straight for the Shuttle. Andy Allen was alone at the controls when the radar sounded a collision alarm. He couldn't see the satellite because they were on the dark side of the earth and he couldn't get a fix from his instruments because it was so close.

Immediately he fired the reaction-control jets, using valuable propellant that would be needed to get the ship in the right attitude for re-entry. But that seemed a long way off. Avoiding a crash was more important, so he kept on firing the jets until eventually a crew member saw the satellite and everyone could work out which way to turn. The two craft came within 700 feet of each other.

So, we marvel then at the skill of the crews and at the technological challenges that NASA has had to overcome. But do we ever stop and wonder what on earth the Space Shuttle is actually for?

It was conceived in the early seventies and announced on 5 January 1972 by Richard Nixon. He said the Shuttle would transform the frontier of space in the seventies into familiar territory, easily accessible for human endeavour in the eighties and nineties. This wasn't a lie. But it did turn out to be wrong.

Originally the plan was for 50 launches a year – nearly one a week – and even as recently as 1985 they were talking about one a fortnight. But they seriously underestimated the time it would take to turn a Shuttle round between missions. I mean, if it lands at Edwards Air Force Base in California, it must be fastened to the back of a Boeing 747 and flown back to Florida at a cost of $750,000. Because of the time and expense of everything, they never really fly more than six or seven times a year.

There was another problem too. The inference of Nixon's speech was that soon normal people would be going into space, not just a bunch of white, college-educated American males. But unfortunately the white, college-educated American males didn't really hold with this. The astronauts felt that if females and plumbers were allowed up there, their status would be eroded. If a plumber can do it . . .

Eventually they agreed that civilians could come along, and selected a 37-year-old schoolteacher, Christa McAuliffe. She was plucked from 11,000 applicants, spent a year in training and on 28 January 1986 was

The pilot has got to slow the machine down from 17,000 mph to a safe landing speed of 211 mph. This is tricky, partly because he has no fuel left and therefore no power and partly because the Shuttle has the aerodynamic properties of an Aga. As a result, he has to make a series of sweeping turns, washing off speed with each one, but even then the rate of descent is still seven times greater than in a normal plane.

TO PENETRATE THE EARTH'S ATMOSPHERE, THE NOSE CONE HAS TO WITHSTAND A SHOCKWAVE THAT, AT 3,000 DEGREES FAHRENHEIT, IS CONSIDERABLY HOTTER THAN THE SURFACE OF THE SUN.

strapped into *Challenger*. Just 74 seconds after take-off an O-ring on the fuel tank broke, and television viewers around the world were treated to the unedifying sight of a Space Shuttle exploding.

I was in a Fulham pub when the pictures were flashed onto a TV screen above the bar and I remember the whole place fell absolutely silent. Never again, we thought, will any of us see anything quite so violent and quite so shocking. Little did we realise, of course, that on 11 September 2001 we would ...

The *Challenger* accident was a catastrophe for NASA, and not only because it killed seven people. It was a catastrophe because it didn't destroy just one Shuttle. It seriously damaged all of them.

Suddenly the public realised that space travel was not and could never be routine. So the Nixon dream of people popping up there 'for a laugh', so to speak, suddenly seemed very far away. And worse, corporate satellites were banned from the cargo area so NASA would never again be exposed to commercial pressure. The military had never been fans of the Shuttle so suddenly it looked like a delivery truck with nothing to deliver, a Shuttle with nowhere to shuttle to. It looked like it was doomed.

When operations began again two and a half years later I had no idea what they were doing. It seemed like the crews were going up there, eating Phenergan to settle their sicky tummies and then coming back again. They teamed up with the Russians so they could use the Mir Space Station as a stopping-off point, but mostly it all seemed rather pointless.

It still does actually. Sure, in November 1998 they finally got the first piece of the International Space Station into orbit and the Shuttle became a vital part of that programme. But then came the re-entry loss of *Columbia*, which broke apart 200,000 feet over Texas, and that grounded them again.

Bush may say that Mars is the next goal but Bush is an idiot. Now everyone is more interested in genetic blueprints and human cloning than space travel.

So here we are. We've already colonised the bit of space that surrounds our planet and we've already been to the Moon, which is a useless lump of rock. To progress, we have to start thinking about the moons of Jupiter and the next galaxy, and that means we're going to need far more power than we have now.

It seems to me, then, that today the Shuttle is nothing more than a stopgap, a device that keeps our hand in while we think what to do next.

Each time it takes off its enormous power serves only to demonstrate that, really, it's nowhere near powerful enough. So, far from being a reminder of how brilliant we are, the poor thing merely reminds us that when it comes to the exploration of space we're puny and absolutely hopeless.

GT40

It was quite a con. I'd managed to convince the producers of 'old' *Top Gear* that we should film a feature about fast Fords through the ages.

The suits nodded sagely as their new-boy presenter outlined his treatment. We would have a look at cars such as the Cortina 1600E and the Escort RS2000, which would bring a sense of teary nostalgia to the piece, and then we'd look at the new Fiesta turbo for the 'yoof' audience. 'Everyone likes a fast Ford,' I argued, and they agreed, giving me the green light to set it up.

I'd given them the sort of marketing speak that TV types love, but actually there was only one reason I wanted to look at souped-up Fords past and present: because it'd mean I'd achieve a dream. I'd get to drive the fastest Ford of them all – the GT40.

The day arrived and I went through the motions of being excited at the XR3s and the Consul GTs. They'd all been brought along by proud owners who were almost priapic at the notion of having their cars on television, so it would have been churlish to have pointed out that they were merely extras, a bit of padding leading up to the great event.

I'd loved the GT40 since I was six. At that time Ferraris were so exotic and so alien that there seemed little point in worrying about them. I was living in Doncaster, so I was never going to even see one for heaven's sake. Whereas Fords were different. I mean, my dad had one of those.

So when I heard that a Ford was going to Le Mans to take on these exotic alien space ships from Italy I could sense, even then, that David was loading his sling in readiness for the battle with Goliath. What I didn't know then is that the GT40 had been born out of spite.

In the early sixties Ford had been on the verge of buying Ferrari but at the last minute, worried that his beloved race team would be drowned by big-company bureaucracy, Enzo had pulled out of the deal. Henry Ford was so livid at the public rebuttal that he ordered his enormous empire to build a car that would go to Le Mans and make Ferrari look like a team of part-time amateurs.

The Americans initially offered up a 4.2-litre V8 that produced 350 bhp and a top speed of 207 mph. But this was deemed too wet so it was increased in size to 4.7 litres. And that didn't work either.

THE GT40 INITIALLY HAD A 4.2-LITRE V8 THAT PRODUCED 350 BHP AND A TOP SPEED OF 207 MPH. BUT THIS WAS DEEMED TOO WET SO IT WAS INCREASED IN SIZE TO 4.7 LITRES.

The early prototypes were nose-light, tail-happy, unreliable dogs but, driven by his need to humiliate Enzo Ferrari, Henry Ford ploughed on. The British team working on the chassis and body, which was 40 inches tall hence the GT40 name, fiddled with aerodynamics and the complexities of fitting a spare wheel under the stubby bonnet. The Americans meanwhile worked on the engine, eventually going the whole hog and coming up with a massive 7-litre V8.

This did the trick and in 1966 Ford won the greatest race of them all. And not just once either but four times on the trot. Here, then, was a blue-collar street fighter beating a blue-blooded aristocrat. It made a little boy in Doncaster very happy indeed because, so far as I was concerned, it was my dad's Anglia out there, doing the business.

And now, nearly thirty years later, I was about to climb into a real GT40 and take it for a spin.

It wasn't a racer. It was one of the seven road cars built by Ford to commemorate the victories. There were plans for more, but a road test in a respected American car magazine was critical, saying the detuned V8 with just 300 bhp on tap was not gutsy enough and that,

When I heard that a Ford was going to Le Mans to take on these exotic alien space ships from Italy I could sense that David was loading his sling in readiness for the battle with Goliath.

with its big boot on the back, the car was ugly. Ford was incensed and the road project was canned.

I didn't care though. I was about to drive a dream and as I opened that low, low door my heart was beating like a washing machine full of wellingtons.

I got one leg inside and knew I was in trouble. It didn't really slide under the dashboard as I'd imagined. So I took it out again and went in backside first, but that didn't work either. Eventually, with much huffing and puffing, I did get my feet onto the pedals and my bum into the seat, but then the door wouldn't close because my head was in the way. I had the car. I had the keys. I had the right insurance. But I was just too tall. It was a crushing blow.

In some ways, though, it was a good thing. They say you should never meet your heroes because they will always be a disappointment. True: when I was four Johnny Morris told me to 'bugger off' when I asked for his autograph. And I think it's the same with cars.

The simple fact of the matter is that the road-going GT40 is slower, more uncomfortable, less safe, less well equipped than, say, a Golf GTi, and nowhere near as nice to drive. Had I been able to take it for a spin I would have been let down. And that would probably have been worse than not being able to get inside.

So what about the new GT, built to celebrate Ford's centenary. Although it can't be called a GT40, because Ford sold the rights to the name to a kit-car company, it does look like one. Bigger, yes, and sharper round the edges, but there's no mistaking the shape. It's beautiful, and brutal and wonderful.

But unlike the old car, this one is spacious, easy to drive and extraordinarily fast. With a 5.4-litre V8 engine, lifted straight from the Lightning pickup truck, you get 540 lbs feet of torque, 540 bhp and as a result a top speed of 212 mph. That makes it not only faster than the GT40 but faster than any other road car on the market today. The blue-collar, Bruce Springsteen heart still beats.

THE CHASSIS AND BODY WAS JUST 40 INCHES TALL, HENCE THE GT 40 NAME.

Happily, I'm due to get one and I'm sure we'll have many happy miles together. But when all is said and done it is a fake, a facsimile of the real thing.

I shall enjoy the car in the garage. But I love the one in the poster above my desk.

YAMATO

248

It was an Italian engineer who first came up with the notion of a battleship. Vittorio Cuniberti reasoned way back in 1903 that soon naval vessels would not only have to face attack from the surface. Torpedoes would make them vulnerable from below and, who knows, one day bombs could be dropped by 'aero craft' making ships susceptible from above as well.

His solution was simple. The modern ship, he reckoned, would have to be fast, supremely well armoured and fitted only with massive guns. No more pea-shooters for close-range stuff. Just lots and lots of monsters.

This way, the battleship could use its speed to get to the right place while its armour resisted any attack from above or below. And then, when it was correctly positioned, the enemy could be bombarded with a hail of 12-inch – or better still 16-inch – shells.

There was no point fitting smaller supplementary guns. The splashes made when their shells missed the target would obscure the view for the main armament and make life difficult for the loaders in the magazines. If there was only one type of shell in there, the chance of sending the wrong type to the wrong gun was eliminated.

Sound military reasoning, I'm sure you'll agree. But there was another advantage to such a huge and powerful ship. Prestige. Let the world know you have a 'battleship' and suddenly you are a force to be reckoned with.

Japan was the first nation to start building such a thing but, inevitably, it was the British who got theirs into the water first. It was constructed in just 100 days, it was christened by King Edward VII and it would give its name to every battleship that ever there was.

It was called HMS *Dreadnought*.

This 17,900-ton monster was protected with armour eleven inches thick and bristled with ten 12-inch guns. That she could move at all was astonishing. That she could do 21 knots was phenomenal. But she could because she was the first large warship ever to be fitted with a steam turbine – a new device that extracted the energy of dry, superheated steam as mechanical movement.

At the time Britannia ruled the waves. Everyone had known that for two hundred years. But *Dreadnought* was something else. *Dreadnought* turned the Royal Navy from a formidable fighting force that could have taken on the navies of France and Russia, at the same time, into something that could have taken on the world.

Unfortunately, for Britain at least, other countries had also adopted Cuniberti's ideas. They included Japan, America, Brazil, New Zealand, Argentina, Russia, Turkey, Chile, France and, most worrying of all, Germany.

Germany had made it plain that its battle fleet would be so strong that 'even the adversary with the greatest sea power' – that would be us – 'would be loath to take it on'.

Germany had a big advantage too. Its fleet only needed to prowl around in the Baltic and the North Sea, so the ship designers didn't need to worry about storage for food and fuel, or crew comfort – they'd only be at sea for short periods. British battleships, on the other hand, had to cover an area extending from Hong Kong and Australasia through every ocean on earth. That meant our crews would be away for months so we had to 'waste' space on larders and beds. This made the Royal Navy ships unbelievably expensive. *Dreadnought* had cost £2 million. Ten years later its sisters were costing £3 million and the only way was up.

Such was the value of our dreadnoughts that Navy commanders had to think up new tactics for using them. In the past they had attacked and killed, and then attacked again. But such was the firepower of the enemy's new battleships, and such was the cost of ours, that they had to start thinking about defence.

And not just defence from other battleships either. One puny little mine or one nasty little torpedo could sink these enormous gun platforms if it got past the armour.

There was a psychological issue too. If the Navy had lost a dreadnought, the effect on morale back at home would have been catastrophic. You could have told the British Tommy that his wife was ugly or that he had a small willy and he wouldn't have minded. But sink one of his battleships and he'd crumple, a broken and disconsolate man.

HMS *Dreadnought*
was constructed in just
100 days, was christened
by King Edward VII and
would give its name
to every battleship
that ever there was.

The result was simple. In the new Navy, with its new big ships, attack became a dirty word. Defence was everything.

So, when the First World War erupted our ships hung around their home base. And the Germans? Well they didn't much want to risk their dreadnoughts either so they too stayed close to home. For the first couple of war years all that happened in the North Sea were brief, high-speed forays by minelayers.

And then came Jutland, in which the cheaper, less well-armed and armoured battlecruisers from both navies beat the hell out of each other. As the smoke blew away, the giant dreadnoughts were in range and the scene was set for the world's first battleship battle. It didn't happen though because the German commander decided a victory would have been good but not *that* important in the scheme of things, whereas a defeat would have been utterly catastrophic. So, he ordered his fleet to turn for home. And run.

His opposite number from the Royal Navy could have given chase. We had more, better, faster ships but he was fearful the Germans might have laid mines in their wake. So he too turned away. The result was astonishing. In the entire course of the First World War not a single battleship was sunk by another battleship.

After hostilities were ended the German fleet was scuppered and a treaty drawn up to limit the size of battleships in the future. This lasted for, ooh, about twenty minutes. Then everyone started gearing up for Round 2.

By now there were several variations on a theme. Some battleships were coming along with almost no armour at all to make them fast. Some had a protective shell only where it mattered. Others were iron clad from prow to stern. There was much debate on what type of guns should be fitted too and, more importantly, where they should go. The British decided at one point that they wouldn't have any at the back 'because we do not run away', but actually there was a sound reason for this.

If you have guns fore and aft, you need to turn the ship sideways so they can all be brought to bear on a target. And a ship that's sideways on to the enemy is a juicy target. If all its guns are at the front, the ship is much harder to hit.

Sounds sensible. And it was, but the British Navy did have one disadvantage over all the others. We had tradition. There was a sense in the Senior Service that 'we do it this way because we always have'. Rate of fire was considered more important, for instance, than accuracy. Because rate of fire is what had won the day at Trafalgar.

Still, as the Second World War kicked off we were still a force to be reckoned with on the high seas. Unfortunately, the Germans had pretty much caught up again. And so, at 5 a.m. on 24 May 1941, began one of the most famous and disastrous naval battles of all time.

The battleship KMS *Bismarck* had been dispatched to the North Atlantic by German High Command to destroy as many merchant ships as possible. As was the way with battleships, the captain had been ordered to avoid at all costs any British warships. They really didn't want their pride and joy damaged.

But the British couldn't allow such a killing machine to roam around the Atlantic at will, disrupting the vital supply lines from America. And since the only way to stop a battleship was with another, we had to bite the bullet so to speak.

The *Bismarck* was located and shadowed by four cruisers, none of which could do much to stop it. So they kept their distance until our big guns rolled up. The big guns in question were the battleship HMS *Prince of Wales* and the battlecruiser HMS *Hood*.

Hood fired first from its two forward turrets but stupidly it was aiming at the *Bismarck*'s escort ship. The *Prince of Wales* got the right target but missed. The German escort ship fired back, hitting the *Hood* but not badly. Then the British fired again, and again and again. A good rate of fire, but lousy accuracy. All of the shots missed.

And then it was the *Bismarck*'s turn. Its first salvo also missed, and it must have seemed at this point that the outcome would be decided on which ships were the toughest and which navy had the most accurate guns. One thing was for sure; this was to be a long day.

American battleship
USS *New Jersey* fires
a broadside with all nine
of her 16-inch guns.

But it wasn't. On just its fifth salvo the *Bismarck* hit the *Hood*, which blew up, split in two and within three minutes had sunk. All but three of its 1,419 crew were killed.

Then the *Bismarck* turned its fearsome armoury on the *Prince of Wales*, which was hit and damaged. It turned away from the fight.

For the first time a battleship had proved its worth in a battle. But in doing so it had also exposed its biggest weakness . . . It could never, in a thousand years, be allowed to get away with it.

Back at home Churchill knew what effect the destruction of the *Hood* would have on morale. Yes, the loss of life had been horrific, but the loss of the ship was somehow worse. The *Hood* had been a battlecruiser rather than a battleship, but it was the pride of the fleet nevertheless because it was still a dreadnought. Even the Germans on board *Bismarck* had been scared of it.

So the Royal Navy was ordered to find the *Bismarck* and extract some payback. The damaged *Prince of Wales* tracked the mighty German while the most extraordinary hunting party was assembled. The battlecruiser *Renown*, the aircraft carrier *Ark Royal* and the cruiser *Sheffield* were dispatched from Gibraltar. The battleship *Ramillies* was released from convoy-escort duties and the *Rodney*, with its forward-facing guns, was sent from its station just off Ireland.

Then you had the original search party, which was also ordered to seek and destroy. The battleship *King George V*, the fleet carrier *Victorious* and the battlecruiser *Repulse*.

All that . . . to get one ship.

The first attack from a torpedo-carrying Swordfish biplane failed to dent the enormous battleship and the second was even more useless, since it was launched in error against the British ship *Sheffield*. But the third struck home and the *Bismarck*'s rudder was damaged.

Helplessly steaming in circles, the poor old thing could only wait for the pack to descend, and descend they did, like a pack of wolves.

Early on the morning of 27 May the *King George V* and the *Rodney* opened fire, and in 90 minutes turned the enemy into an inferno. But still she wouldn't sink. So torpedoes were launched from the heavy

The battleship had to be fast, supremely well armoured and fitted only with massive guns. No more pea-shooters for close-range stuff. Just lots and lots of monsters.

cruiser *Dorsetshire*, which had been called in as well the previous day, to finish her off. The pride of the German Navy sank at 10.36 a.m. just off Ireland.

She was killed but I don't think this could be called a defeat. I mean, she had killed first, taking out one of the most-loved ships in the Royal Navy, and then she had tied up a simply enormous amount of the British fleet for days.

When it came to wasting the enemy's time though, *Bismarck*'s sister ship, the *Tirpitz*, was even more successful.

Fourteen times the Royal Air Force launched massive bombing raids to destroy her while she was still being built. But none was successful and on 25 February 1941 she was commissioned into service.

Just three months later the *Bismarck* was sunk and the Germans had to think hard about the role of their new big boy. They decided when she became operational in January 1942 that they really couldn't afford to lose her. So she was sent to Norway, where she spent most of the war hiding in a fjord.

Sounds pathetic, but there was method in their madness. They knew the British and the Russians couldn't afford to just ignore the hulking presence. They knew the Allies would stop at nothing to get her, and that this would tie up a simply vast amount of resources. Resources that otherwise might be used in the Atlantic or the Mediterranean.

This was the joy of a battleship. It was more of a prize than Hitler himself.

The plan worked like a dream. Just two weeks after she first arrived in Norway, seven Stirlings and nine Halifaxes were sent in on bombing raids. Poor weather caused the attack to be aborted. The weather also caused another, much larger raid to be halted two months later. But in April the skies were clear enough for 30 Halifaxes and 11 Lancasters to get through. The ship escaped unharmed. And it wasn't scratched the next night either when 32 British planes attacked.

The attacks then stopped so the *Tirpitz* nosed out of the fjord and went in search of convoys. Almost immediately a Russian submarine pounced and slammed a torpedo into her side with such force that the crew on board said they never felt a thing. Happily, she failed to find any merchant ships to destroy but this foray did at least remind the British she was still around.

In October we were back with a plan to use human torpedoes. But this went awry in the North Sea so we tried again with midget submarines, using six big subs to tow them over there. They did manage to lay mines under her keel and two went off with devastating force. A normal ship would have succumbed to the blasts but *Tirpitz* was not normal. Yes, her hull was damaged and, yes, there was severe damage to her rudders and turbines. But she remained afloat.

While she was being repaired the Russians mounted an air raid, which was unsuccessful, and then it was our turn to get serious. On 3 April 1944 41 Barracudas swooped out of the sky and this time, finally, an air raid worked. Fifteen bombs hit home. Incredibly, though, *Tirpitz* survived this and the next three air raids and just three months later put to sea.

For two months we threw just about everything at the damn thing until eventually, in October, a Lancaster found the bow with a bomb and *Tirpitz* was brought to her knees. With her top speed down to just ten knots she headed for the protection of Norway where, on 12 November 1944, 31 Lancasters using Tallboy bombs blew her to pieces.

She listed to port and rolled over so quickly that nearly 1,000 men were drowned.

And then just three years after the war finished she was bought by a salvage company for a mere 100,000 Norwegian Kroner and broken up for scrap. A sad end for a ship that sank nothing but possibly tied up more resources than any single weapon in the history of warfare.

I'd like to say *Tirpitz* was the greatest of all the battleships. But I think the best has to be the biggest. The *Yamato*.

Tirpitz had weighed 41,000 tons and was considered to be vast. *Yamato* weighed 68,000 tons and that's just hyperbolic.

She was a tough old bird too with armour plating eight inches thick in weak places and a full 22 inches thick where it mattered. In fact her armour alone weighed more than the total weight of the world's

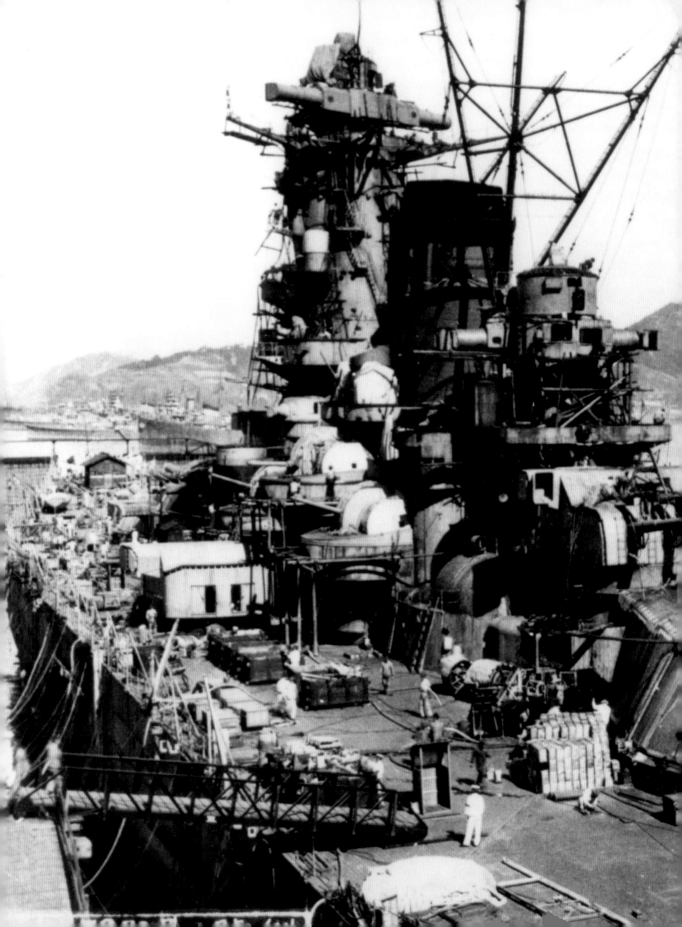

Yamato had 141 anti-aircraft guns. But these were an *amuse bouche* compared to her main 18-inch weapons, which were simply humungous. Each one could fire a 1.3-ton shell 25 miles. Yup, that's right. 1.3 tons and 25 miles. And she had nine of them.

YAMATO WEIGHED 68,000 TONS AND THATS JUST HYPERBOLIC. HER ARMOUR ALONE WEIGHED MORE THAN THE TOTAL WEIGHT OF THE WORLD'S SECOND-BIGGEST BATTLESHIP.

second-biggest battleship. This was her *raison d'être*. To startle and shock and terrify. We had a ship called the *Invincible*. They had a ship that really was.

She was Japan's third island, with 1,147 compartments. She was so big that she could and did carry seven aircraft. And yet despite all this size and weight, she could blat along at 27 knots. That's faster than most modern jet skis.

Oh, and to protect her from air attack while she was busy pounding the main enemy to pieces she had 141 anti-aircraft guns.

But these were an *amuse bouche* compared to her main 18-inch weapons, which were simply humungous. Each one could fire a 1.3-ton shell 25 miles. Yup, that's right. 1.3 tons and 25 miles. And she had nine of them.

Now the British had once mounted one gun of this size on the *Furious*. But it was always felt that it would do more damage to the ship from which it was fired than the ship it was aiming at.

One of the crew members on *Furious* remembers a test firing, saying, 'I think it had a range of something like 30 miles and I don't imagine it would ever have found the right target but it was certainly very spectacular. The recoil was tremendous. Every time she fired it was like a snowstorm in my cabin but instead of snowflakes it was sheared rivet heads coming down from the deckhead and partition.'

In other words, one 18-inch gun used to tear the *Furious* apart every time it was fired. And remember, the *Yamato* had nine. NINE!

Once I stood next to a tank that fired its miserable shell and the blast damn nearly knocked me off me feet. So God alone knows what it would have been like if the pride of Japan's navy had ever fired all its main guns at once. They'd have heard the roar on the other side of the world. There'd have been tsunamis and hurricanes. It would have been biblical. Real, genuine ocean-parting ferocity. And then some.

And what would the recoil have done when twelve tons of high explosive was launched out of those barrels? She was built by Mitsubishi but it's hard to imagine even their legendary build-quality was up to the task.

Then there was the man in charge of this awesome firepower, Admiral Yamamoto, a man who didn't like the war. He was immortalised in *Tora! Tora! Tora!* and again in *Pearl Harbor* as the old sage who said, 'I fear all we have done is awaken a sleeping giant.'

He also didn't like battleships, realising that while they could tie up an enemy they weren't much good at fighting for all the wrong reasons: i.e., they cost too much.

Sure enough, his massive charge had a fairly undistinguished war, cruising around the Pacific a lot and mostly staying out of harm's way. Her moment of triumph, the moment when she was elevated to greatness, came on 7 April 1945, during an operation called Ten Go. It was an operation designed specifically to kill her and it was mounted by the Japanese themselves.

By this stage the war was lost. The US forces had reached Okin awa and *Yamato* was the only big ship Japan's navy had left. So she was given just enough fuel for a one-way trip and ordered out on a suicide mission against the invading Americans.

The Americans knew it was coming and were well aware by then just how devastating kamikaze raids could be. So they took the threat seriously, sending no fewer than 400 aircraft to deal with it. And in case this failed, six battleships were put on standby as well.

In the course of the war, the Americans had torpedoed the *Yamato* once, but little damage was done. They'd bombed it too, with even less effect. They had also been on the receiving end of those gigantic guns so they knew full well it wasn't going to be stopped easily. But even in their wildest dreams they couldn't have imagined how much punishment this truly breathtaking ship would take.

The carrier-based planes quickly took out the *Yamato*'s little escort ships and in the next hour hit the main prize with a staggering twenty torpedoes. And still she sailed on, bringing her 141 anti-aircraft guns to bear. Only after she'd been hit by seventeen heavy bombs did she finally roll to port and explode. Beneath a mushroom cloud 1,000 feet tall the greatest battleship ever built sank in two pieces in 1,000 feet of water.

Very quickly after the war people began to question the wisdom of these dreadnoughts. Few had been lost to fire from other battleships and the number of ships they'd sunk was minimal. They'd been used to bombard shore defences, but frankly aircraft carriers were much better at that sort of thing.

And so it was that aircraft carriers became the new flagships.

The last British battleship, HMS *Vanguard*, was removed from service in 1960, while the Americans hung on gamely until 1998 before turning their last one, the USS *Missouri*, into a floating museum off Hawaii. Today there are none.

This is sad, because I've been on a Nimitz Class carrier, and while its nuclear power plant only needs refuelling once every millennium and its planes can reach targets even further away than a battleship's guns and it can do an amazing 33 knots it's a bit of a brute. Ugly too.

And that's a charge that could never be laid at the door of the battleship, especially the *Yamato*.

Some might say that no machine conceived only to kill could ever be called beautiful. Magnificent maybe, and awesome perhaps. But not beautiful. The thing is though that in the battleship's short life of just 90 years it turned out to be a less effective killing machine than almost any other weapon of war. All they did was steam around the oceans, making the people who paid for them feel good.

So I do consider them beautiful and I consider *Yamato* to be the most beautiful of them all.

SPITFIRE

In 1940 everything was tickety-boo for the Germans. They'd strolled into Poland and France, Belgium, Holland, Luxembourg, Norway, Denmark and Czechoslovakia with no real problem at all and almost certainly thought the British would be another walkover. Mop us up. Bish bash bosh. And off we go to Moscow. Unfortunately, however, their plans were spoiled by one thing.

Since the Second World War ended – and we won by the way – pundits have queued up to explain what, in their opinion, was the single most important weapon in the arsenal that brought us victory. Patton said it was the Willys Jeep. Many scientists say it was the invention of radar. The Great British public like to heap praise on the drunken Kurd-killer, Winston Churchill. Me though? I think it was the Spitfire.

Aaaargh, say those of a planespotting disposition. It is impossible, say the anoraks, to single out one fighter from this period as 'the best'. The P-51 Mustang, they argue, had a far greater range than the Spit and, in 1942, the pride of the Royal Air Force was definitely outclassed and outgunned by the Focke-Wulf 190.

Then there are those who claim that, actually, since there were more Hurricanes than Spitfires in the War this was the plane that won the Battle of Britain and therefore meant our little island could be used as a springboard by the Americans in 1944. Yes, they say, the Hurricane was the one true champion. The greatest of the great. The finger in the dyke that held back the menace of Nazism.

Bollocks. The only reason why we're free to discuss the matter in books and internet chat rooms is because of Reginald Mitchell's Spit.

Reg worked for a company called Supermarine, which before the war made all sorts of ungainly flying machines like the Walrus. However, the company was also heavily involved in the fabled Schneider Trophy. Established in 1913, it was effectively an international race for seaplanes.

A simple concept but flawed, because the instigator, Frenchman Jacques Schneider, said that if one country won the event three times on the trot, the Trophy would be theirs for good. Well, Supermarine won it for Britain in 1927, then again in 1928 and then again, in front of 250,000 spectators, in 1929.

In doing so, the company learned a great deal about aerodynamics while Rolls-Royce, who made the engines, learned all about superchargers and power. So, when the government finally realised Germany was becoming a threat, and decided to give the RAF some new fighters to replace their ageing biplanes, Supermarine was in an ideal position to help out.

The company had been founded by a genuine British hero, Noel Pemberton-Billing. He was a yachtsman and racing driver, and decided in 1913 he should learn to fly. But being double barrelled, he wasn't going to take his time. In fact he bet a friend £500 he could get an aviator's licence not in a day – but before breakfast. And he did.

However, it was his chief designer, Reginald Mitchell, who came up with the Shrew, or the Shrike. Two names that were considered before everyone agreed that it'd be better if the new plane was called Spitfire.

I'd love to say at this point that he drew a vague shape in the sand while walking on a beach and the world's greatest fighter was born. But in fact it was one of the most complicated and difficult labours in the history of aviation.

Famously, the first pilot ever to fly the prototype climbed out afterwards and said, 'I don't want anything touched.' History has taught us that he meant he was perfectly happy with the performance but this wasn't so. He was actually telling his ground crew not to change any of the components so that he could do another test in the same circumstances later. Actually, the plane was a bit of a dog.

Half the problem was that, despite the lessons learned in seaplane racing, and despite the astonishing 27-litre Merlin engine, it just wasn't fast enough.

After a great deal of fettling and tweaking they got it up to 335 mph, but this was only 5 mph faster than Hawker's much simpler and cheaper Hurricane. So, being British, the engineers took their pipes to the potting shed and realised that the propeller's tips were encountering Mach problems. They were changed and whoomph – the speed shot up to 348 mph.

A still from the 1969 film
The Battle of Britain.

Great, but the new-found speed was likely to be lost on production Spitfires since they would be held together not with the smooth rivets used on the prototype but with cheaper dome-headed rivets. To find out what effect this would have, they glued split peas to the wings and fuselage. That is the most British example of ingenuity I know.

It turned out that when the peas were fastened in place, the speed fell by a staggering and totally unacceptable 22 mph. But providing they were arranged in straight lines, the aerodynamics remained unaffected and so did the precious top speed.

Better still, Rolls-Royce were beavering away with the engine. They found that by pointing the exhaust outlets backwards they could use ejected gases to provide 70 lb of thrust. The speed increased again, to 380 mph.

But as the performance increased, more problems came along, chief among which was the death of the Spitfire's creator, Mitchell, from cancer, at the age of 42.

He left his colleagues with an inspired design that was riddled with difficulties. For instance, the rear-facing exhausts glowed red, and with the blue flames coming out of them the pilot couldn't see a damn thing after sunset.

Then there were the problems of starting the Merlin, oil-consumption, 'float' just before the plane landed, and 'Spitfire Knuckle', which was caused when pilots were pumping the undercarriage down by hand. Worst of all, there was a chronic shortage of headroom. Early Spitfires had a flat canopy. Only later models came with a bubble.

And then there were issues with altitude. The prototype Spit had reached 37,000 feet, which is the same height you reach on your way to Barbados today. Fine. But this far up, the guns froze. You pulled the trigger and . . . nothing.

Worse, as you came down they thawed out so that when you hit the ground even the mildest jolt would release a single round. Worrying for the ground crews.

Months were spent trying to get heat from the engine into the wings, to stop the Brownings seizing up.

It may have been hard to create the Spitfire but the finished product was demonstrably better than anything the Nazis sent our way. In essence, the Spit could climb, turn and fly faster than a Messerschmitt. More importantly, when an Me109 reached its ceiling the Spit had 3,000 feet in hand. And height, in a dogfight, is everything.

BETWEEN JULY AND OCTOBER IN 1940 747 SPITFIRES WERE DELIVERED, 361 WERE DESTROYED AND 352 DAMAGED.

And then there was the difficulty of actually making a Spitfire. Unlike the Hurricane, it was a monocoque with a stressed skin, which required specialist production techniques. Worse, because it was felt the plane couldn't be made in a single factory – what if it were to be bombed? – the government approached Lord Nuffield, the car boss, to ask if his Castle Bromwich plant would be available. He agreed but, even though war was imminent, the workforce did not, and responded in the only way the Brummies know how – with a series of industrial disputes.

Eventually the government became so weary of the problems in Birmingham they took control of the factory from an astonished Nuffield and gave it to Supermarine's new owners at Vickers. The Spitfire was in business and all for a cost to the taxpayer of just £12,478. Has there ever been a better deal?

The list of countries queuing up to buy this amazing new plane was astonishing. Every air force in the world wanted a go. Cheekily, even the Japanese sent in an order – for just one. I wonder what they were going to do with it. In fact only one was exported, to France, before the War began.

It may have been hard to create the Spitfire but the finished product was demonstrably better than anything the Nazis sent our way. In essence, the Spit could climb, turn and fly faster than a Messerschmitt. More importantly, when an Me109 reached its ceiling the Spit had 3,000 feet in hand. And height, in a dogfight, is everything.

Yes, the Me109 had fuel injection, which meant the engine would work even when the plane was pulling negative g, whereas the Spit's Merlin used carburettors that ceased to provide fuel if the g-meter started reading a minus figure.

Sadly though, the first two planes shot down by Spitfires in the Second World War were Hurricanes.

Eventually fighter command sorted itself out, the radar stations came on stream and the Battle of Britain was underway.

It was agreed that the Hurricanes should go after bombers, leaving the Spitfires to take care of the Messerschmitt fighter escorts. But having read several accounts of what life was like in a dogfight, I know this was a nonsensical notion.

You dived down on the German formations, picked a target, fired a very short burst, and then found yourself miles from the action, twisting and turning to make sure no one was on your tail. Occasionally you'd encounter another plane and have another pop at it, but more often you'd lose sight of the battle completely. And then run low on fuel.

The notion that you could dive into the pack and worry about what sort of plane you should be shooting at is just plain silly. I can't even do that on a pleasant day's pheasant shooting. Often we're told to shoot cocks only, but I find this almost impossible and regularly hit hens as well, along with a selection of owls, buzzards and songbirds. And that's when I'm standing still. The notion of being able to determine the sex of a bird while running around a field at top speed is laughable.

Something else that's laughable is the idea that 'our young men had to shoot down their young men at the rate of four to one'. In fact by the second week of the Battle of Britain we had more Spits and

The fact is simple. The Spitfire looked good. It was every bit as dashing as the young men who flew it, and in flight it was as graceful as any bird. Its progress through the sky seemed effortless, as though it was simply riding the breeze and its Merlin engine was only there to provide a suitable soundtrack.

THE MARK IX HAD A 37-LITRE, 2,050-HORSEPOWER ENGINE WITH A TWO-SPEED, TWO-STAGE SUPERCHARGER, A FIVE-BLADED PROPELLER, TWO CANNONS AND FOUR MACHINE GUNS, AND IT COULD FLY FOR 850 MILES AT SPEEDS UP TO 450 MPH.

Hurricanes than we did when the War started. Between July and October in 1940 747 Spitfires were delivered, 361 were destroyed and 352 damaged.

Yes, there was always a shortage of good pilots, but with plenty of Poles and Canadians flocking to Britain at this time it wasn't as acute as you may have been led to believe.

So, on 15 September Germany launched its biggest attack yet. 200 bombers were launched against London. Even though they were protected by fighter escorts, 52 never made it back again. And the number of Spitfires lost? Seven. That night Hitler postponed his plans to invade Britain indefinitely.

A year later, however, the Luftwaffe took delivery of the Focke-Wulf 190, which was better than the Spitfire in every respect. Had the Germans been equipped with this when the War started we'd have lost; it's that simple. It was so good in fact that Churchill called an immediate halt to all fighter operations over Northern Europe.

But the Nazi advantage was short-lived because in 1943 the Spitfire Mark IX was introduced. It had a 37-litre, 2,050-horsepower engine with a two-speed, two-stage supercharger, a five-bladed propeller, two cannons and four machine guns, and it could fly for 850 miles at speeds up to 450 mph. More than 5,000 Mark IXs were made and suddenly the Germans' FW190 looked like a horse and cart.

And this was the beauty of Mitchell's original design. It was almost as though he'd realised that the first incarnation would need to be updated over and over again, and it was. They were used on aircraft carriers, they were used in streamlined form for photo-reconnaissance, they were turned into ground-attack mud movers. One Spitfire even reached a speed of 680 mph. It became the RAF's Swiss-Army knife.

The last time the Spit was used in a military operation was 1963. There was trouble in Indonesia, where the locals were still using old propeller-driven Mustangs. So to see how these would stack up against a modern jet fighter, the RAF staged a duel between their new Mach 2 Lightning and an old Spitfire.

Although the Lightning crew always had the option of lighting the burners and getting the hell out of Dodge, it was discovered that in a turning dogfight the Spit would get some rounds into its tormentor.

So, the Spitfire was more than just a good plane. It started out as a great plane and, having seen off the Nazis in 1940, became better and better and better.

However, those with plenty of time on their hands have found that statistically it was no better in action than the Hurricane. Both had an equal chance of victory.

Perhaps the Hurricane was a great plane too. From a pilot's point of view it was certainly easier to fly and it was a better gun platform. From a government's point of view it was cheaper to buy than the £6,000 Spitfire and easier to mend. But from the point of view of those on the ground, the poor souls on the receiving end of all those German bombs, it was the Spitfire that won their hearts.

Technically, the Hurricane might have been able to win the Battle of Britain on its own. But for keeping up the spirits of the people on the ground while running rings round anything the Third Reich could throw at it? That was the job of the Spitfire, a symbol of British brilliance, a symbol of hope.

The fact is simple. The Spitfire looked good. It was every bit as dashing as the young men who flew it, and in flight it was as graceful as any bird. Its progress through the sky seemed effortless, as though it was simply riding the breeze and its Merlin engine was only there to provide a suitable soundtrack.

You had Mr Churchill on the radio explaining that we'd never surrender, and above you had the Spitfire, and you couldn't help thinking: Yes, we can win this thing.

Possibly, just possibly, the Spitfire is the greatest machine ever made.

Possibly, just possibly,
the Spitfire is the greatest
machine ever made.

PICTURE CREDITS